SHOW ME MISSOURI POLITICS

★ ★ ★ ★ ★ ★

A Guidebook to the Missouri Constitution

★ ★ ★ Robynn Kuhlmann

University of Central Missouri

Kendall Hunt
publishing company

Kendall Hunt
publishing company

www.kendallhunt.com
Send all inquiries to:
4050 Westmark Drive
Dubuque, IA 52004-1840

Printed in the United States of America

CONTENTS

Chapter 1

MISSOURI POLITICAL CULTURE

★ Introduction

Constitutions are roadmaps to set up a system of governance. They determine powers between governmental branches and also the relationship between citizens and government. Such documents are contracts between citizens and the state, not only defining what government cannot do, but also what government *should* do. These written documents, among other things, are foundational in understanding, establishing, and perpetuating certain *political cultures.* Political cultures are the general attitudes of citizens about the role of government and the citizen's role in it. It is "rooted in the historical experiences of groups of people" and affects the way the people interact with government and the way they think government should interact with citizens.[1] In some ways, geography, shared history, and economic elements help to shape this. It can have an effect on a variety of policy outputs, voting habits, taxing and spending, and other political behaviors and phenomenon. In the case of the United States, as a whole, individualism, liberty, equality, and self-governance are all base components of American political culture. While Americans share similar values, each state has some variation in how citizens view government and their own role in it. It is no secret that Missouri has a mixture of political cultures that makes it unique on its own. This chapter is aimed at providing an overview of Missouri's regional differences in political culture, geography, and the economy. These aspects can make a difference in the political atmosphere and help to explain why Missourians have unique political values.

Missouri

© illpos/Shutterstock.com

Missouri's Political Culture

Some citizens believe that government should not play an active role in solving some issues, while others may believe that it should. Similarly, some citizens may argue that they, as citizens, should play a more active role in politics, while others believe that it is best left to elected officials. These are the beliefs and attitudes about the role of government and its citizens in the governmental process—a facet of a particular type of political culture.

Although Americans share similar values and attitudes, they may vary quite a bit from region to region. Since the United States is larger than the size of Western Europe, and comprises of a variety of backgrounds and geographic histories, it makes sense that there are regional differences in how U.S. citizens view the role of government and their role in the governmental process. Individuals living on the coast of California, for example, may have different views about the role of government in regulating guns than people who are living in Missouri. Based on this view, many Californians may be fine with having some of the strictest gun laws in the United States. Meanwhile, Missouri has fairly lax gun laws. Why are there these differences? Like much of the Midwest, many Missourians have had experiences with a long tradition of using guns for sports and recreation. However, urban dwellers may associate guns with violence, while those living in rural areas may associate guns with good times vacationing with the family during hunting trips—a source of bonding between family members.

As one can see, lifestyles and traditions for citizens vary across the American states. Missouri has a unique political culture of its own. Missouri's political culture is known as a mixture between *individualistic* and *traditionalistic* political cultures that political scientist Daniel Elazar identified. Set out to find differences between American political culture and European political cultures, Elazar found that there were three political cultures in the United States—moralistic, individualistic, and traditionalistic.

Moralistic political cultures are associated with states in the region of the Great Lakes and parts of the Midwest and Western states, but not Missouri. Citizens in this political culture see government as something positive. Citizens should work with government to advance public interests and solve problems. Corruption in government is not viewed as the norm and is not tolerated. With this view, citizens are expected to participate in politics and emphasize cooperation among other citizens to do the same. Often, in these states, political scientists observe higher levels of political participation such as voting.

In individualistic political cultures, citizens see politics as a market place to solve problems. Government is thought of as an instrument for citizens to use. Overall, government should have a limited role and should only act when called upon by citizens. The individualistic political culture is associated with Anglo and German immigrants—and the swath of early German and Scottish settlers in Missouri may have greatly affected this.

We can see streaks of individualistic political cultures by observing the most mundane and divisive aspects of Missouri politics. Political scientist Richard Dom points out that the large number of small local governments compared to the size of the Missouri population is evidence of the individualistic political culture in practice.[2] This coincides with the idea that government should not be too big and out of the peoples reach when they need to use it. While the number of governments per populous may not be a very well-known or interesting feature of Missouri's individualistic political culture, what is apparent is Missourians reluctance to expand governments role, even if many citizens would not be directly affected. One recent example is when the citizens of Missouri had a choice to increase the tax on tobacco via Proposition B, the 2012 Tobacco Tax Initiative. Missouri is one among 24 states that has what is called *direct democracy,* where citizens vote directly to change laws. Laws in which citizens can directly vote on are called *initiatives* (also known as *propositions*). This is different than voting for representatives who serve in legislatures who vote on laws on behalf of the citizens, which is called a *republic* or *representative government.* Missouri is a republic in the U.S. representative governmental system, but also has components of direct democracy. If Missourians voted to pass the 2012 Tobacco Tax Initiative, it would have created a Health and Education Trust Fund with the money that was generated on a 73 cent increase on a pack of cigarettes (along with tax increases on other tobacco products).

This money would have gone to the Missouri public school system and initiated tobacco use cessation programs in the state. Although narrowly defeated, it is no wonder it was—in individualistic political cultures this initiative may be seen as a move to increase the role of government. In a survey conducted on a tobacco tax increase years prior to Proposition B, the most cited reason Missourians said they opposed this type of initiative was because they "did not trust the government to spend the tax revenues as intended…".[3] This is a prime example of the state's nick-name, 'The Show Me State,' as citizens are generally skeptical of government activities.

Did you know?...

Legends of Missouri as the "Show Me State"

Missouri is termed as the "Show Me State" and one legend attributes this to U.S. Representative Willard Duncan Vandiver, a Missouri Congressman who served in Congress from 1897–1903. During a speech he stated "I come from a state that raises corn and cotton and cockleburs and Democrats, and frothy eloquence neither convinces nor satisfies me. I am from Missouri. You have got to show me." It is also attributed to Missouri miners that filled a gap during a mining strike in Colorado. Since the Missourian miners were unfamiliar with the mining practices legend holds that Coloradoan pit bosses stated that they were from Missouri, you'll have to show them.[4]

Missouri also has a traditionalistic political culture. In traditionalistic political cultures there is a sort of ambivalent or tentative attitude toward politics. Ordinary citizens are not supposed to take part in politics and it is generally up to those who have traditionally held political office to rule. Political elites should make the decisions in government. Many political elites have traditionally been family members of individuals who have served in office over the course of generations—a sort of political dynasty. Further, in traditionalistic political cultures, government is supposed to serve to maintain the existing social and economic order. The traditionalistic political culture stems from settlers in the southern portions of the United States. Their focus was on agriculture and the maintenance of plantations. Similarly, much of southern Missouri and many parts of rural Missouri are within the definition of being traditionalistic. One example of Missouri's traditionalistic political culture in some regions is again pointed out by political scientist Richard Dohm. He argues that in counties that once had large slave populations, there is a commitment to keep members of political families in political office. He also points out that many of these candidates run on their connection to the region, not on what they would achieve if they were to win.[5]

Why is there a mixture of political cultures in Missouri? Much of this has to do with migration patterns and the geographic position of the state. More than likely, you are already well aware that northern Missouri is much different than southern Missouri. Just as Kansas City is much different than places such as Lake of the Ozarks or even Springfield, just by visiting can tell you that there are important geographic and economic differences. In fact, traditionalistic political cultures are associated with the southern regions of Missouri and more individualistic political cultures are associated with northern regions of Missouri. Students in Missouri state politics often note that they see a distinct difference in Missouri's political culture above and below Interstate 70—an east to west highway system that virtually splits the middle of Missouri in half. However, Missouri may be best described as a mixture of both with concentrations of traditionalistic political cultures in the south and individualistic political cultures in the north and areas with a combination of these two political cultures in the same region.

Population and Diverse Social Systems

Missouri's population was estimated at 6,063,589 by the U.S. Census in 2015. This ranks Missouri as 18th in population size among all U.S. states. However, population growth is declining in Missouri where its ranking slipped from the 15th most populous state in 1990 to the 18th most populous state in the 2010 U.S. Census. Why is there interest in population growth and decline if studying politics? One reason is that population can equate to a healthy workforce. As people age, it is important to have younger populations take the place of those who are no longer able to work due to age, or who have decided to retire. A population decline also means that there is less money going towards government functions through taxes. A healthy tax base means that state funds can be used for roads to be paved, public education, and the salaries for police officers, firemen, and other public service workers. In terms of population size, the largest three counties in Missouri are St. Louis County, Jackson County, and Greene County. The smallest three counties in Missouri are Mercer, Knox, and Shuyler counties.[6]

Citizens and politicians alike are interested in a healthy economy. And if the economy is not going very well in a state, it can affect voting patterns, views of government, the behaviors of politicians, and the types of policies that are created in a state. One example is Iowa. Due to population loss, Iowa Governor Tom Vilsack tried to woo immigrants into the state and declared Iowa as the "Ellis Island of the Midwest."[7] Missouri's declining population also has many politicians moving to swoon people to the state. With St. Louis projected to have the largest decline in population in the state by 2030, St. Louis Mayor Francis Slay publically sought high skilled immigrants to move into the city.

The racial and ethnic make-up of Missouri can also affect politics and policy. Missouri is fairly diverse. Known as the 'Gateway to the West' the state had attracted a variety of groups early on in the territories history. German, Irish, and Scottish immigrants gave Missouri a fairly diverse population early on. Many who migrated from Kentucky, Tennessee, Virginia, and North Carolina also brought African American slaves. The slave population

© Bill Fehr/Shutterstock.com

Missouri is the Gateway to the West

in the Missouri territory grew from 14% of the total population of 20,845 individuals in 1810, to 18% of a total 141,024 individuals in the state by 1840.[8] By 1860, Missouri slaves accounted for about 9.7% of the total population.[9] From 1810 to 1860, there was an estimated 281% increase in the number of African American slaves in Missouri. Many of the African American slaves were populated along the Missouri and Mississippi rivers, where slave owners settled due to rich soil for their crops. After the Civil War in 1865, the war in the United States that abolished slavery, many African Americans began to flee north out of southern states due to lynching, harassment, and attempts at financial and political deprivation. There was a large out-migration of African Americans to northern and Midwestern states during the 1870s. This added to the number of African Americans in the state of Missouri. In 2013, the estimated population of African Americans in Missouri was 11.7% compared to Whites who make up 82.8% of the total Missouri population. While 11.7% may not seem like much, concentrations of African Americans are high in certain regions. For example, according to the 2010 U.S. Census, the top three areas for concentrations of African Americans were the city of St. Louis at 49.2%, and the counties of Pemiscot, Mississippi, and Jackson at about 25%. Racial minorities in Missouri also include those with Hispanic or Latino descent, who make up 3.5% of the states' population. More recently, since the 1990's, some towns that have food processing companies are argued to have attracted Latino populations. Sullivan County for example has a Hispanic population that constitutes 18.2% of the population. These populations create pockets of diverse social systems in the state of Missouri.

Did you know?...

Black Migration—the Kansas Exodus

In the 1870s many black southerners focused on migrating to Kansas. This was because the state was seen as a place where they could live and work freely due to the efforts of John Brown, a leading abolitionist in the state of Kansas. This migration to the Midwestern and northern states were so noticeable that the U.S. Senate created a special committee to investigate the causes.[10]

Racial diversity can affect politics in many ways. While states with high immigrant populations may impose restrictions such as English only laws, other states or regions may encounter issues surrounding racial inequality. The protests and riots that made national headlines following the shooting of a black teenager, Michael Brown, by a white police officer in the city of Ferguson, Missouri, brought to surface some of the civil rights issues that African Americans had historically encountered. The ensuing 2015 report by the federal governments' Department of Justice outlined that racial discrimination was deeply embedded in local government agencies including the police force in Ferguson. These reports have caused some public officials to step down from their positions.

Regional Differences—Shaping Politics through Natural Resources and Industry

There are other regional differences in Missouri that are connected to industrial development and natural resources that also have an effect on politics. Missouri has a number of natural resources and a very diverse economy. In fact, the state of Missouri is ranked as being the 4th most diverse economy in the United States.[11] This diverse economy has been credited with insulating Missouri from the 2008 economic recession.[12]

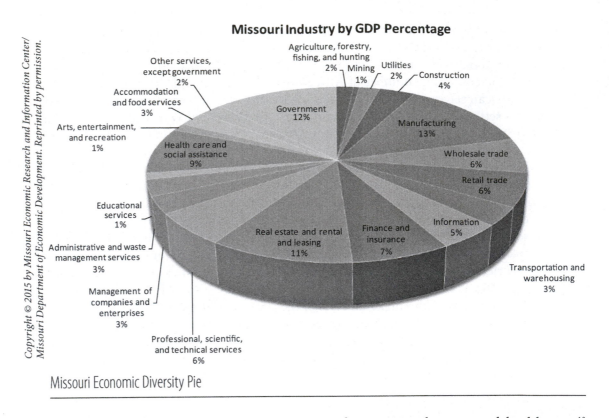

Missouri Economic Diversity Pie

The top three industries in Missouri are manufacturing, real estate, and health care.[13] Combined, these three industries make up 33% of Missouri's highly diversified economy. Manufacturing is the top industry in Missouri and within that category, the top three manufacturing industries are in food, transportation, and fabricated metal.[14] Missouri has a healthy industrial footing in aerospace and defense, and have contracts with the U.S. federal government. Missouri also has mines and in 2013 ranked 9th in the value of nonfuel mineral production in the United States.[15] These minerals include portland stone for cement, lead, lime, sand, and gravel. Missouri is the top producer of lead, with six mines primarily located in central, southwest, and southeast Missouri.[16] As for transportation, chemical manufacturing, and food, the largest importers of these goods are Canada and Mexico. Other countries that import Missouri goods are China, Japan, Indonesia, and India.[17] This requires trade relations between Missouri, other states, and countries. The largest growing sector, though, is food processing where companies can take advantage of Missouri's home grown agriculture and livestock.

Although agriculture does not take up much of the *gross domestic product* of the state, that is, the total monetary value of all the goods and services in Missouri, it certainly has a presence. Missouri is located in a region of the United States that is considered to be the *farm belt*. The farm belt is where most of the country's large scale farming occurs. Missouri has an excellent tradition of farming a variety of food sources as well as raising livestock. These include soybeans, corn, and wheat. Livestock includes beef, pork, and chicken. According to the U.S. Census Bureau, Missouri ranks within the top 15 states for output of these agricultural products. The presence of agriculture in the state of Missouri, indeed affects its' politics. When bills concerning agriculture are considered at the state legislature, representatives of the Missouri Farm Bureau, for example, often testify at hearings. More recent discussions concerning opening up Cuba to U.S. markets, has certainly shook up Missouri politics. President Barack Obama announced plans to open up trade with Cuba, a country that had been sanctioned from U.S. goods due to its undemocratic regime. Democrat Missouri Senator Claire McCaskill praised the move in hopes of exporting Missouri's agricultural products. Alternatively, Missouri republican Senator Roy Blunt chastised the policy arguing that normalizing relations with Cuba reinforces a regime that has historically suppressed civil liberties.

Religion and Political Ideology

Missouri's distinct location in the middle of the country places it in both the farm belt, but also, the *Bible Belt*. The Bible Belt consists of much of the middle and southern portions of the United States. This includes many southern states such as Tennessee, Kentucky, Georgia, Mississippi, Louisiana, Arkansas, and Texas. The northern portion of the Bible Belt includes Missouri, Kansas, Iowa, Nebraska, South Dakota, and North Dakota. In the Bible Belt there are many more Christian adherents than in other regions of the country. Further, the Bible Belt region also tends to be more *conservative* rather than *liberal*. These are types of *political ideologies* which are consistent patterns of beliefs about the proper course and scope of government.

Conservatives in the United States tend to want less government intervention in the economy and to focus on promoting traditional family values associated with Christianity. These are values that promote marriage between a man and a woman. This also encompasses traditional gender roles that encourage females to work at home raising their children while males work outside the home. On the economic side, they tend to believe that the government should not be highly involved in distribution of welfare and this reflects their stance on keeping taxes low. States in the Bible Belt have high church attendance and citizens can be heavily influenced by their religious views. In these states you will see that discussion about issues such as abortion and gay marriage take on a religious tone and religion being utilized as the primary argument against these two.

Liberals tend to believe in using government to promote conditions of equality and do not tend to view politics through a religious lens. The most socially liberal states are states on west coast and northeast. They are likely to favor gay marriage, abortion, and positive government action in welfare. They generally see the right to abortions as an issue of equality and believe that women have a right to choose to have one or not. Similar to the issue of abortion, gay marriage is viewed as an issue of equality. Liberal individuals will more than likely believe that everyone should have a right to marry, not just heterosexual couples.

According to Gallup, a polling agency, the state of Missouri is above average in the percentages of conservatives. Gallup's State of the States survey illustrated that almost 40% of Missourians identify as conservative, while about 18% identify as liberal and 37% identify as being politically *moderate*, that is, people who do not identify themselves as being in the extreme spectrums of conservative or liberal.[18] Although there are a good amount of Missourians who identify as moderate, there is a healthy percentage who are conservative. Additionally, a similar proportion of Missourians say they are "very religious"—43%—while 30% say they are moderately religious. This leaves just a little over a quarter of Missouri's population identifying as non-religious.

Protestors for the Ban on Same-sex Marriage

© Benjamin F. Haith/Shutterstock.com

The conservative and religious make-up of Missouri certainly affects its' political landscape. Even though same-sex marriage was already banned in 1996, in 2004, the citizens of Missouri voted on a ballot initiative, Constitutional Amendment 2, which would again ban same-sex marriage in the state of Missouri. Not surprisingly, 71% of those who turned out

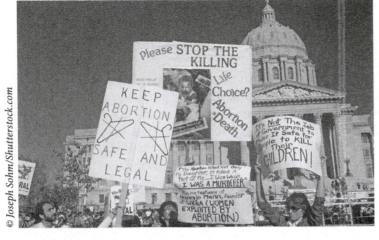

Pro-Life Protestors

to vote in the state voted to ban same sex marriage. The arguments for this ban in the state were centered on religious values. Backing the ban, then spokeswoman for the Coalition to Protect Marriage in Missouri, and current Missouri Representative Vicki Hartzler reflected this stance by saying "I'm hopeful we will be able to send a very strong, clear message from Missouri that here in the heartland, we value traditional marriage."[19]

Another issue area that reflects the religious and conservative make-up of Missouri is the issue of abortion. Missouri has some of the tightest restrictions on abortions in the United States. Generally, states that have more Christian adherents are more likely to have stricter abortion regulations. According to the Guttmacher Institute, Missouri is within the top five states with the most restrictions in obtaining an abortion. In Missouri, women must receive counseling 72 hours prior to receiving an abortion, abortions are only covered under private insurance unless the pregnancy threatens the life of the woman, and minors must receive parental consent. In 2015, a Missouri state legislator introduced a bill that would only allow women to receive abortions under the condition that they had written permission from the man that contributed to the pregnancy. These policies certainly reflect the conservative leanings of citizens in Missouri as well as the states' placement in the Bible Belt.

Missouri in the U.S. System

Although Americans share similar values such as liberty, equality, and self-governance, there are some differences in how they view what their role in government should be and what government should do. Missouri's unique political cultures are both individualistic and traditionalistic—which are influenced by the migration patterns of early Anglo, German, and Scottish settlers. The individualistic political culture makes many Missourians tentative about expanding the role of government in their state. The traditionalistic political culture of the state also helps to maintain the existing political structure. Situated in the bible belt and with its' conservative and moderate political leanings, citizens in the state of Missouri reflect the values of neighboring states and this can affect policies such as same-sex marriage and abortion. These are all aspects that can affect the political behaviors of citizens, as well as politicians in the state. Missouri has a diverse economy and is situated in the farm belt. It makes the state prime for trade agreements between other states and even other countries. This can also affect what Missouri politicians do in office. Certainly, politicians should take notice of what could benefit the economy of Missouri and create or continue policies based the rich agricultural products of Missouri.

Missouri's diverse population also helps to shape politics. The history of racial migration for African Americans, either unwillingly through the slave trade, or willingly through inspiration of freedom, helps us to understand why events such as racial discord in Ferguson, for example, can occur. Interestingly, aspects of the state such as food processing companies can draw more racial diversity into the state. The more recent influx of Hispanic immigrants due to the economic opportunities that the food processing industry provides may have Missouri politicians focusing on policies concerning immigration, and even perhaps workers conditions.

★ KEY TERMS ★

Moralistic
Direct Democracy
Initiatives
Propositions
Republic

Representative Government
Gross Domestic Product
Farm Belt
Bible Belt

Political Ideologies
Conservative
Liberal
Moderate

★ ENDNOTES ★

[1] Elazar, Daniel. *American Federalism: A View from the States.* 2nd Ed. Cromwell, 1972. Print.

[2] Hardy, Richard J., Richard R.Dohm, and David A. Leuthold. *Missouri Government and Politics.* Columbia: University of Missouri Press, 1995. Print.

[3] Knapp, Timothy D., and Gary D. Brinker. "Missouri Voter's Opinions on Tobacco Taxation: Survey of Registered Voters." Center for Social Science and Public Policy Research: Missouri State University, 2007.

[4] Rossiter, Phyllis. "I'm from Missouri—you'll have to show me." *Rural Missouri,* 42:3, 1989. Also see Official Manual of the State of Missouri, 1979–1980, page 1486.

[5] Hardy, Richard J., Richard R. Dohm, and David A. Leuthold.*Missouri Government and Politics.* Columbia: University of Missouri Press, 1995. Print.

[6] Missouri Office of Administration: Division of Planning and Budget. "Population Projections—Total Populations Missouri Counties 2000–2030." March 12th 2015, http://archive.oa.mo.gov/bp/projections/TotalPop.pdf.

[7] Longworth, Richard C. "Caught in the Middle: America's heartland in the Age of Globalism." Bloomsbury: New York, 2007.

[8] Texler, Harrison Anthony. "Slavery in Missouri, 1804–1865." Thesis. Baltimore: John Hopkins Press, 1914.

[9] Ibid

[10] Davis, Damani. 2008. "Exodus to Kansas: The 1880 Senate Investigation of the Beginnings of the African American Migration from the South." National Archives, Prologue Magazine 40:2.

[11] Missouri Economic and Research Center. 2015. Missouri Economic Indicator Brief: *Missouri Economic Diversity. Missouri* Department of Economic Development. Accessed February 24th, 2015. Available at: http://www.missourieconomy.org/pdfs/edi2013_brief.pdf

[12] Ibid.

[13] Ibid.

[14] Missouri Economic and Information Research Center. Missouri Economic Indicator Brief: *Manufacturing Industries.* Accessed February 24th, 2015. Available at: http://www.missourieconomy.org/pdfs/2013_manufacturing_brief.pdf

[15] U.S. Department of Interior. 2013. Mineral Commodity Summaries 2013. U.S. Geological Survey, Reston Virginia. Accessed February 24th, 2015. Available at: http://minerals.usgs.gov/minerals/pubs/mcs/2013/mcs2013.pdf

[16] Ibid.

[17] Ibid.

[18] See Gallup's State of the State series at http://www.gallup.com/poll/114073/state-states-series.aspx

[19] Wiese, Kelly. 2004. Missouri First of Several States to Vote on Gay Marriage Ban this Year. Associated Press. August 2nd, 2004.

Chapter 2

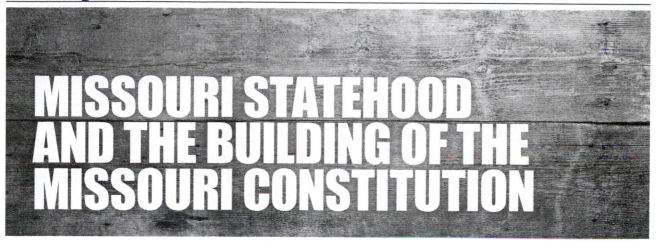

★ Introduction

One of the first documented mentions of what we know now as Missouri was by Western Europeans. In the 1670s, the French planned to explore the area in search of the Mississippi river.[1] It was during the time the British had already acquired American territories east of the Mississippi river. These British territories later developed into the original 13 American colonies and the beginning of the formation of the United States in our modern times. When thinking about land occupied by Western Europeans during this period, it is important to point out that the system of government was very different from what we have today in the United States. Territories and states can have differences in who wields power and how much autonomy government has in those jurisdictions. A *territory* is an area that is under the rule of a higher political body, and has no autonomous government within it. A *state* is a geographic area with defined borders and an organized political system that may or may not have a higher authority, but, is autonomous in its' own way. Before an organized political system was developed in Missouri, it was a territory where rule over the land changed hands a few times before it became part of the United States. Until the early 1800's Missouri had no real standing as an organized political system.

Missouri's road to statehood under the jurisdiction of Americans has been an interesting and bumpy one. This territory had changed hands a few times from French rule to Spanish rule, to a very short period of French rule again. Finally, it was purchased by the United States in 1803, known as the *Louisiana Purchase*. The eventual adoption of the territory has a rich history and is riddled with plenty of political actors and personalities that can make for an excellent docudrama. The purpose of this chapter is to familiarize readers with a brief history of Missouri as a territory in the 1670s and Missouri's road to statehood in 1821. This chapter also includes a brief overview of the inception of the Missouri constitution in 1820 and compares its' structure and basic differences to the U.S. Constitution.

Missouri (1670s–1803)

French explorers first came across the territory of Missouri in the 1670s. The men who travelled across the area were hired out by the French government to explore the expansive Mississippi river. Those who were hired to explore the area had goals that were two-fold: to find a port (later founded as New Orleans); and to spread Christianity among American-Indians along the way.[3] During the first expedition of these hired guns, the men travelled south from northern territories of French Canada through Missouri and stopped short of their goal in what is known today as Arkansas. In fear of coming across Spanish explorers, who were also fielding the land, the members of the French expeditionary team retreated back north. They only went as far south as Arkansas. This first exploration by Western Europeans was unsuccessful. They did not complete the goal of finding the mouth of the Mississippi river. However, the French did secure trade with the American Indians they encountered and maintained good relations with them. In the 1680s French explorers tried again to secure the mouth of the Mississippi River. They attempted to do so by sailing a fleet of ships through the Gulf Coast. Still, the French were unsuccessful. The head of this expedition, Sieur de La Salle, missed the prized port. His fleet ended up in Texas. Even though they were, yet again, unsuccessful in finding the Mississippi port; this mistake did help to establish the French's presence in much of the Mississippi Valley territory and portions of Arkansas and Missouri.

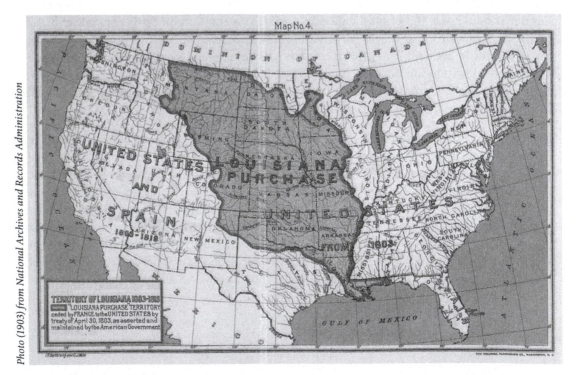

Photo (1903) from National Archives and Records Administration

Map of the Louisiana Purchase

By 1720, the French had claimed territory in areas now known as Missouri, Iowa, Indiana, Wisconsin, Minnesota, Michigan, Ohio, Illinois, Arkansas, Mississippi, Louisiana, Alabama and the north western parts of New York, and Pennsylvania. This area was designated as the *Louisiana Territory*. Still maintaining good relations with the Native Americans, the French received support from them in protecting them from aggressors. By this time, what is now known as the United States was geographically carved up by three European countries. French acquired territory in the middle of America, and the Spanish also had territory in some southern portions, such as Florida and western areas from Texas to California. The British claimed much of the eastern seaboard with American colonies and was beginning to acquire new territories south of it such as North Carolina and South Carolina.

Acquiring territory during this early phase of America was competitive. Missouri's early history is characterized by French maneuvers to gain land in the face of Spanish and British presence. At the same time, American colonists found themselves surrounded by the French and Spanish, who were competing to gain and maintain territory with economic interests in securing it for trade. Eventually, these interests clashed both on American territory and abroad. This clash and gave rise to a series of conflicts and became known as the *French and Indian War* in America, (also known as the Seven Year's War [1754–1763]). In America, the French had support from many Native American tribes, and, near the end of the war had Spain as an ally. However, this was not enough to defeat the British with support from the American colonists. The French and Indian War ended with the British gaining more territory in America and abroad through the signing of the Treaty of Paris in 1763.

Did you know?...

At the age of 21, a very young George Washington spearheaded one of the first battles that sought to stop French settlements in the Ohio Valley. This was the very beginning of the long and bloody French and Indian War.

The outcome of the war included territorial gains for Britain which included areas east of the Mississippi, French Canada, and Florida. As part of a secret agreement, the Louisiana Territory was given to Spain by France in 1762 under the Treaty of Fontainebleau. This meant that the territory of what is now known as Missouri was transferred to Spanish control. Because sending of information was extremely slow as compared to today, word of the transfer of the territory to the Spaniards did not reach occupants of Missouri until 1764. By that time, St. Louis had been established as a new settlement by the French in order to increase economic growth along the Mississippi river. St. Louis became quite a successful port village, and later, a stomping ground for the delegates that wrote the Missouri Constitution and fought for Missouri to gain statehood.

While the Spanish were trying to secure its' newly acquired Louisiana Territory, which included Missouri, the American colonists were growing more and more frustrated with the British King. In an effort to help pay for the French and Indian War, the King of England (King George III) had begun to levy a series of hefty taxes against the American colonies. Most notably, the Stamp Act of 1765 and Townshend Acts of 1767 imposed hefty taxes on the Americans frustrating the colonists due to the economic burden. These taxes were eventually repealed, but a tea tax, among other issues, continued to disgruntle the American colonists. In 1773, this tea tax resulted in the dumping of tea into the Boston harbor by a group of American patriots called the Sons of Liberty, this famous act known as the

The Boston Tea Party

Boston Tea Party. As a result of this defiance, British King George III issued a series of orders known as the Intolerable Acts. The Intolerable Acts included closing the Boston harbor and sending British troops to the American colonies. One may think that closing the Boston harbor may not be all that bad.

However, this closing starved the economic means of Americans who use it for trade and well as receiving goods. By this time, American delegates were already forming ties with each other by addressing their grievances which formally took place in 1774 at the First Continental Congress. When British soldiers and American minutemen clashed in 1775, known as the 'shot that was heard round the world,' the precipice of the beginning American Revolution was reached.[4] This event, among others, spurred the Americans to cut ties through drafting the Declaration of Independence which was formulated at a meeting of delegates during the Second Continental Congress.[5] The Declaration of Independence was signed by colonial delegates in 1776 and laid out the grievances of the Americans against the British monarchy. This document legitimized the reasoning behind dissolving the political relationship between Americans and the British. The first two paragraphs of the Declaration of Independence illustrate the reasoning behind the revolt while the rest is a list of grievances to support the argument for the revolt:

> *"When in the Course of human events, it becomes necessary for one people to dissolve the political bands which have connected them with another, and to assume among the powers of the earth, the separate and equal station to which the Laws of Nature and of Nature's God entitle them, a decent respect to the opinions of mankind requires that they should declare the causes which impel them to the separation.*
>
> *We hold these truths to be self-evident, that all men are created equal, that they are endowed by their Creator with certain unalienable Rights, that among these are Life, Liberty and the pursuit of Happiness.—That to secure these rights, Governments are instituted among Men, deriving their just powers from the consent of the governed,—That whenever any Form of Government becomes destructive of these ends, it is the Right of the People to alter or to abolish it, and to institute new Government, laying its foundation on such principles and organizing its powers in such form, as to them shall seem most likely to effect their Safety and Happiness."*

The Declaration of Independence formalized the American Revolution. Through the declaration, the American colonies declared themselves as *states*. These states all had formal political systems and were considered to be *sovereign* and independent. By claiming sovereignty means that they were not bound to any other higher authority—they were independent political jurisdictions with political systems of their own. One can think of them as having a status of a small country. Of course, Missouri was not included in this revolution because it was still a territory under the rule of the Spanish.

Because the Americans were revolting against the British, a force that had defeated them in the past, the Spanish became allies of the American revolutionaries. Just because Missouri was, in effect, so geographically far from the American states on the east coast, this does not mean that it was impervious to British attacks during the American Revolution. In an effort to regain territory lost during the American Revolution, Britain planned attacks on St. Louis. This was no surprise. Spain, now an American ally, ended up declaring war on Britain during the revolution. On May 26th, 1780, the British, along with Native American allies stormed St. Louis, but it was thwarted by the Spaniards. St. Louis, along with the Louisiana Territory remained in Spanish hands.

The Spanish remained in control of the Louisiana Territory through the creation of the United States Constitution in 1787 and its' ratification in 1789. In the meantime, many Americans were increasingly

The red, white, and blue stripes of the Missouri state flag illustrate the influence of French presence.

starting to settle west of the established American states, closer to and within Spanish Louisiana territory. During this period, the Americans had also allied with the French who were going through their own revolution for self-governance. Although the Spanish remained in control of government functions in the Louisiana Territory until 1803, the French reacquired it through a treaty with Spain in 1800.[6] Just three years later, in 1803, the Louisiana territory was purchased by the United States from France through the efforts of then President Thomas Jefferson. This purchase, now dubbed the *Louisiana Purchase* doubled the size of the United States and began another turn in the road to Missouri's statehood.

Missouri's Road to Statehood (1803–1821)

Missouri was part of the 1803 Louisiana Purchase. This large territory was divided into two sections for the purpose of governmental functions. Recall, that this territory was rather large and includes what we know today as Louisiana, Arkansas, Oklahoma, Kansas, Missouri, South Dakota, and Iowa, as well as parts of Texas, Colorado, Wyoming, Montana, North Dakota, and Minnesota. South of Missouri, right at today's Arkansas-Missouri state line, was designated by the U.S. Congress as the District of New Orleans. Above that state line (which includes Missouri) was designated as the District of Louisiana.[7] U.S. Congress designed a governmental structure over these districts so that there was a presiding Governor and a court system that held executive, legislative, and judicial powers. The District of Louisiana was under the control of the already existing government of Indiana Territory. Under this new form of government, many inhabitants in Missouri were concerned over the lack of established guidelines over *self-governance*—the ability to make their own laws. Another issue was the question as to whether or not slavery was to remain legal.

Delegates in the Missouri territory ended up sending letters to U.S. Congress over their concerns of representation. A petition was drawn up in St. Louis and the petitioners declared themselves as the "Representatives of the District of Louisiana."[8] This newly formed group of individuals had already started to form a government of their own. They created a convention after they found out that U.S. Congress had placed them under the jurisdiction of the District of Louisiana.[9] The first government these Missouri delegates advocated was a sort of military rule. In 1804, then president Thomas Jefferson, rejected the Missouri delegates plans. Eventually, the petitioners received their wishes of more control over government. The District of Louisiana was then designated as the Louisiana Territory. Power was transferred to a Governor and judges appointed by the President of the United States, which had the same broad legislative and judicial powers as the government of the Indiana Territory.[10]

From 1800 to 1810 the population in the Missouri territory grew rapidly. U.S. Congress had established guidelines based on the size of the population in which territories could apply for statehood. By 1810, numerous petitions to have a state government system in Missouri were being sent to U.S. Congress. It was not until 1812 that Congress officially changed the name of the area to the Territory of Missouri, which granted them more autonomy in governing, but still, not the full status of a state. This new status, though, did give citizens in Missouri the ability to form a legislature and have a representative in U.S. Congress. Because of this new status, the legislature of the Territory of Missouri had representatives elected by the citizens of the territory as well as a Legal Council whose members were appointed by the President of the United States. This means that power welded in one of the first Missouri legislatures was split between representatives selected by citizens and representatives selected by U.S. government. By 1817, representatives of the state of Missouri along with citizens sent numerous petitions to U.S. Congress to garner statehood. If declared a state, its' citizens as well as existing government officials would have more control over Missouri government functions.

The question as to under what circumstances the Territory of Missouri would become a state recognized by U.S. government became known as the famous *Missouri Question*. When U.S. Congress was considering Missouri statehood, an amendment was proposed that Missouri would become a free state, meaning that all African Americans born after admittance into the United States would be free and not subject to slavery. This issue gave rise to a number of objections and fired-up discourse over the issue of slavery in the United States. It troubled then ex-President Thomas Jefferson so much that in a private letter he wrote: "this mementous question, like a fire bell in the night, awakened and filled me with terror."[11] Jefferson's words foreshadowed a dark period of American history—the fight over abolishing slavery in the United States.

At the same time the Missouri question was being considered, Maine was petitioning for statehood. U.S. Congress initially tied both petitions together. Efforts by some congressmen to take out the provision that Missouri would be a free state failed, and the debate went back and forth between U.S. representatives for two Congressional sessions. In 1820, Congress finally passed legislation that gave Missouri its' statehood which would be finalized in 1821. With this passage was a compromise—the Missouri Compromise. The *Missouri Compromise* stipulated that Missouri would be admitted as a slave state and all states above an imaginary line north of latitude 36 30 of the Louisiana Purchase would remain non-slave states. Maine was admitted to the United States as a free-state.

The Missouri Constitution and Missouri's Constitutional Structure

While the Missouri Question was being debated in U.S. Congress in 1820, Missouri's constitutional convention was taking place in St. Louis. Recall that constitutions are roadmaps to set up a system of governance. They determine the powers between governmental branches and also the relationship between citizens and government. Constitutions are contracts between citizens and the state, and define what government cannot do, but also what government *should* do. The men at Missouri's constitutional convention were not starting from scratch. There was an embedded history of over 40 years of states that have had existing constitutions in the American political system. There was also 200 years of a semi-democratic rule since the formation of the first U.S. colonies. By 1820, 22 states had already entered into the union of the United States. There was certainly much to draw from while building the Missouri Constitution.

In effect, including the U.S. Constitution, there were 23 examples for the founding fathers of the Missouri constitution to build upon. The Missouri Constitution was written in 38 days. The men who helped in writing the Missouri constitution were highly educated statesmen, mostly coming from families with a long history of wealth and experience in governing and law as well as in agriculture. Just like many states during the colonial period, there already was a culture of some autonomy, or freedom in self-governance. The American tradition of self-governance also included the Madisonian ideal of limited government and the original and ensuing Missouri constitutions reflect these values. In the section on the Declaration of Rights, Article XII, section 1 of the original Missouri Constitution, the principle of self-governance is apparent: "That the general, great, and essential principles of liberty and free government may be recognized and established, we declare….That all political power is vested in, and derived from, the people."

Missouri already had a governor's seat (as an executive), a legislature, and a judicial system. The Missouri constitution was written to formalize an existing government and laid out the powers, duties, and limitations of the governor, legislature, and judicial branches of government. This is similar to the governmental structure of U.S. federal government and all other states. It also formalized a sort of bill of rights for citizens of the state and the limitations of government action of the state of Missouri in relation to its' citizens.

Did you know?...

Many of the men who helped to write the Missouri constitution were not originally from Missouri. Although many were long-time residents of the state, the primary states they came from were Maryland, Virginia, and Kentucky.

The Missouri Constitution was adopted on July 19th, 1820. Since 1820, there have been four Constitutions for the state of Missouri. The first Missouri Constitution was short compared the recent Missouri constitutions. However, the first Missouri constitution was relatively long compared to the U.S. Constitution at the time with 9,220 words compared to 5,430 words in the amended U.S. Constitution in 1820. The Missouri Constitution has grown quite a bit since its original constitution. As of 2014, the length of the Missouri constitution is 69,394 words—above the national average.[12] In line with other state constitutions, a clear separation of powers between government branches is defined. The first article establishes the boundaries of the state of Missouri while the rest of the constitution addresses the distribution of power between three governmental branches; the legislature, executive, and judiciary, and lastly, the Declaration of Rights for state citizens which was inspired by the U.S. Bill of Rights (See Table 1).

Aside from differences in simple order of subject areas, one of the major differences in the first Missouri constitution is that it established a sort of bill of rights within the text of the original constitution—which is a common practice in U.S. state constitutions. However, the difference is that the U.S. Bill of Rights was amended on to the U.S. Constitution in 1791, a few years after its' ratification. Another notable difference in the Missouri Constitution is the inclusion of a clause, Article 3 Section 26. Missouri's constitution included a unique *denial of power*. It did not allow for the Missouri state legislature to pass bills that would free black slaves. This section also required the legislature to pass laws that would ban freed slaves from immigrating into the state and a law to punish white owners for mistreatment of slaves. Because the Missouri Constitution was drafted and ratified before statehood, when presented to members of U.S. Congress, the inclusion of Article 3 Section 26, started

TABLE 1: Comparing Constitutions: U.S. and Missouri in 1820

	1820 Missouri Constitution	U.S. Constitution
Article I	Boundaries of the State of Missouri	Legislative Branch
Article II	Powers are divided into three departments	Executive Branch
Article III	Legislative Branch	Judiciary
Article IV	Executive Branch	Rights and Denials of Power for States; Requirements for Admission to the Union
Article V	Judicial Branch	Procedures for Amending the Constitution
Article VI	Empowers Legislature to Develop Education	Dictates that U.S. National laws are supreme over state laws (Supremacy Clause)

*Articles VII through XII of the first Missouri Constitution include the right for the legislature to have jurisdiction over improvements in roads and waterways, establishing a bank for state funds, procedures for amending the Missouri Constitution. Article XIII is the Declaration of Rights a bill of rights for Missouri citizens.

another heated debate. The *Second Missouri Compromise* ensued—U.S. Congress would only grant statehood to Missouri if its' legislature passed a "solemn public act."[13] The passage of the solemn public act ensured that anyone who was considered a U.S. citizen could legally enter into the state of Missouri. This would ensure that the privileges and immunities clause of the U.S. Constitution would not be violated. The *privileges and immunities clause* in Article 4 of the U.S. Constitution requires that states do not discriminate against citizens of other states.

When comparing the Missouri Constitution to the U.S. Constitution, the Missouri Constitution is much more detailed in particular functions such as in education, roads and waterways, and many other aspects of state government. This is a normal feature of state constitutions. Since states are granted a zone of authority over their territory, they also have the power over the basic functions of government activity such as granting drivers licenses, marriage licenses, imposing a variety taxes, building roads, and many other powers as long as it does not violate national law. Although this zone of authority is limited, which will be discussed in the following chapter, what is granted to states, (at least to a certain extent), can make state constitutions lengthy.

Did you know?...

Did you know that on average state constitutions have 120 amendments? Amendments to the U.S. Constitution pales in relation to state constitutions with only 27 amendments.

Missouri's 4 Constitutions

In all, Missouri has had four constitutions with the latest one ratified in 1945. The second constitution was adopted after the Civil War in 1865. This constitution abolished slavery provisions and was known as the "Drake Constitution" which was also dubbed as "Draconian Code."[14] It was thought of as draconian because it had included provisions that were meant to punish confederate sympathizers and did not allow anyone who helped or fought with the confederates during the Civil War to vote and hold certain positions in Missouri. These include teachers, lawyers, and church officials. In order to have the right to vote, citizens would have to take an "Ironclad Oath," an oath that said they had always been loyal and will remain loyal to the United States and did not take part in helping the confederates. This section of the Drake Constitution was ruled unconstitutional by the U.S Supreme Court and therefore later invalidated.[15]

The Civil War had its toll on Missouri. This picture depicts border counties that were ordered to be evacuated. Many evacuated Missourians came back to destroyed homes.

The third Missouri Constitution was ratified in 1875. This constitution addressed the growing population in the state and local needs. The 1875 constitution allowed for large local governments such as St. Louis to have more say in how to address needs through "home-rule."[16] It also strengthened the governor's branch through longer terms, allowed citizens to vote for Supreme Court Justices, and limited taxation. This constitution was much more detailed than the 1865 Constitution. It became even more so through the initiative process, a direct democracy system which was adopted in 1907. In 1920, Missourians voted to approve a ballot measure that would let them vote on whether they would have a constitutional convention. This measure included the feature that Missourians would be faced with this question every 20 years. When presented with the opportunity to have a constitutional convention, citizens voted for it. Because of voter approval, the current Missouri constitution was ratified in 1945 and streamlined so that many of the amendments were put into statutory law. The current Missouri Constitution of 1945 is different in structure than the 1820 Missouri Constitution, as well as the U.S. Constitution (see Table 2).

There are some other key general differences between the Missouri Constitution and the U.S. Constitution. First, even though the U.S. Constitution and Missouri Constitution designates one executive (the President of U.S. government and a governor of Missouri government), the U.S. president appoints his executive officials. In Missouri these executive officials are elected by citizens of the state. Also, the U.S. legislature is different in size. While there are 535 members of U.S. Congress (435 in the house and 100 in the senate), there are 197 members of the Missouri General Assembly (163 in the house and 34 in the senate). Also, the U.S. Supreme court has nine members while the Missouri Supreme Court has seven members. The difference in how these branches function will be discussed in following chapters.

Another major difference is how the U.S. Constitution and Missouri Constitution allow for their constitutions to be amended, or added to. There are two ways in which the U.S. Constitution can be amended: by ⅔'s a majority vote in both the house and the senate; or ⅔'s of the states call for a constitutional convention and the proposed amendment is approved by ¾'s of the states. In Missouri there are three ways to amend the Missouri Constitution

TABLE 2: Comparing Current Constitutions: U.S. and Missouri

	Current Missouri Constitution	U.S. Constitution
Article I	Bill of Rights	Legislative Branch
Article II	Powers are divided into three departments	Executive Branch
Article III	Legislative Branch	Judiciary
Article IV	Executive Branch	Rights and Denials of Power for States; Requirements for Admission to the Union
Article V	Judicial Branch	Procedures for Amending the Constitution
Article VI	Local Government Power	Dictates that U.S. National laws are supreme over state laws (Supremacy Clause)

and the requirements are not as high. One way is through the state legislature and a legislatively referred referendum. A referendum is when the state legislature proposes a joint resolution to amend the constitution and if approved by a simple majority in both the house and the senate, it will be on the ballot for a popular vote by Missouri citizens. If citizens approve this by a simple majority, the Missouri Constitution will be amended.

Another way is through a popular initiative. A popular initiative is when citizens gather enough signatures to have a proposal placed on the ballot. If a simple majority of citizens vote 'yes' to a proposal to amend the Missouri Constitution, then it will be amended. Lastly, as mentioned in a prior discussion in this chapter, every 20 years Missourians are faced with a question on the ballot as to whether or not to have a state constitutional convention. Although it hasn't occurred since 1942, if approved, then delegates selected by citizens and citizens alike propose amendments during the convention. These amendments are then put up for a popular vote. If approved by a simple majority of voters, then the Missouri Constitution is amended. The next time the citizens of Missouri will face the question as to whether or not to hold a Constitutional convention for Missouri will be in 2022.

These pathways to amend the Missouri constitution set the bar lower than the requirements for amending the U.S. Constitution. Since direct democracy exists in the state of Missouri and there is much more ease in changing the constitution, one can say why it can become so lengthy. As of 2015, Missouri has 60 amendments to the constitution since it was ratified in 1945. This a bit more than twice as many as the 27 amendments the U.S. Constitution has since 1791.

★ Conclusion

The road to statehood for Missouri took almost 150 years since the first French explorers travelled through it in the 1670's. Rule over the territory changed hands a few times and was not impervious to the French Indian War and the American Revolution. In 1803, the United States had the opportunity to purchase it along with a large section of land that almost doubled the size U.S. territory through the Louisiana Purchase. Since the Louisiana Purchase, the citizens of Missouri fought hard to gain the status of a state. Finally, in 1821 Missouri was officially accepted as a state into the union of the United States.

Like many other state constitutions, Missouri's includes a variety of features that makes it different from the U.S. Constitution. At first sight, the most notable difference between the U.S. constitution and all four ensuing constitutions is the order in which it lays out the powers of the branches along with other governmental functions. Although similar to the U.S. Constitution, it lays out the powers of the three branches of government, as well as denials of power of government, and the rights of citizens, the legislative, executive, and judiciary have unique differences in make-up as well as the selection methods of those public officials. Further, the Missouri Constitution is much more detailed than the U.S. Constitution. This is the norm for state constitutions. State constitutions in general, are much more detailed than the U.S. Constitution because they have jurisdiction over a variety of state functions such as education, transportation, and many other areas. Compared to other states, Missouri's Constitution is above average in the amount of detail. This can be attributed to the initiative process and the ease in which the constitution can be amended.

Understanding the differences between the U.S. Constitution and the Missouri Constitution is important. It allows for citizens of the state to navigate a political system in which they are highly affected. This chapter painted the larger picture of the history of Missouri and some broad differences in constitutional design. The following chapters of this book will take on a much more detailed approach—a microscopic view to unveil a better understanding of the Missouri Constitution and Missouri politics.

★ KEY TERMS ★

Territory	Boston Tea Party	Missouri Compromise
State	Sovereign	Second Missouri Compromise
Louisiana Purchase	Self-Governance Missouri	Privileges and Immunities Clause
Louisiana Territory	Question	
French and Indian War		

★ ENDNOTES ★

[1] Foley, William E. The Genesis of Missouri: From Wilderness Outpost to Statehood. 1989. University of Missouri Press.

[2] Ibid

[3] Ibid

[4] Ralph Waldo Emerson wrote the poem, the *Concord Hymn* (1837) to memorialize the 1775 clash between minutemen and the American revolutionaries. The phrase 'the shot heard round the world' is now well known to refer to the political and philosophical principles in which the American Revolution stood.

[5] Although the Declaration of Independence is primarily known to have been authored by Thomas Jefferson, it's earliest form of it was drafted by Richard Henry Lee known as Lee's Resolution. See Shain, Barry Alan. *The Declaration of Independence in Historical Context: American State Papers, Petitions, & Letters of the Delegates to the First National Congress.* 2014. Yale University Press.

6   Shoemaker, Calvin Floyd. *Missouri's Struggle for Statehood 1804-1821.* 1916. Hugh Stephens Printing Co.: Jefferson City, MO.

7   Ibid

8   Ibid, pg 20.

9   Ibid

10 Ibid

11 "From Thomas Jefferson to John Holmes, 22 April 1820," Founders Online, National Archives (http://founders.archives.gov/documents/Jefferson/98-01-02-1234 [last update: 2015-03-20]).

12 Book of the States 2014.The Council of State Governments.

13 See James Monroe: "Proclamation 28—Admitting Missouri to the Union," August 10, 1821. Online by Gerhard Peters and John T. Woolley, *The American Presidency Project.* http://www.presidency.ucsb.edu/ws/?pid=66272.

14 March, David D. "Drake Charles Daniel (1811–1892)" in *Dictionary of Missouri Biography.* 1999. EdsLawerence O. Christensen, William E. Foley, Gary R. Kremer, and Kenneth H. Winn.

15 Cummings v. Missouri (1866).

16 Swindler, William F. 1958. Missouri's Constitutions: History, Theory, and Practice. William and Mary Law School. *Faculty Publications. Paper* 1618. http://scholarship.law.wm.edu/facpubs/1618

17 Fulton, Richard and Jerry Brekke. *Understanding Missouri's Constitutional Government.* 2010. University of Missouri Press: Columbia.

Chapter 3

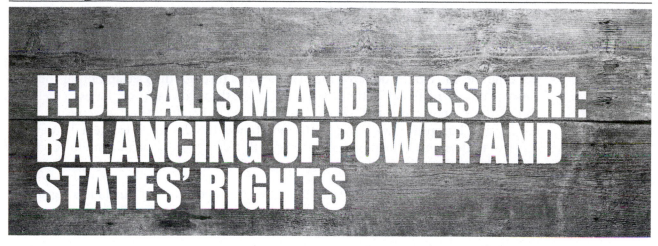

★ Introduction

In 2014, Missouri citizens passed a legislatively referred constitutional amendment to make ownership and possession of a gun an 'unalienable right.' Six months later in January of 2015, this constitutional amendment was interpreted by a St. Louis Circuit Court judge to extend this gun right to all citizens of Missouri.[1] What makes this amendment controversial is that it flies in the face of federal gun laws that ban ex-felons convicted of violent crimes from possessing a firearm. The St. Louis judge interpreted the new amendment to extend to all Missouri citizens regardless of ex-felon status. This is not the only instance in which states have passed laws or amended constitutions that ignore or seek to circumvent federal laws. Legalized use, possession, or sale of marijuana, for example, is also one of them. As of June 2015, 17 states have legalized the use of marijuana for medical purposes. Three states, Colorado, Oregon, and Washington have legalized marijuana for recreational use. Following suit with other states, the dialogue in legalizing marijuana is gaining some ground in Missouri. States are legalizing marijuana despite federal law that makes it a criminal offense to possess, use, or sell it. According to the *supremacy clause* in Article VI of the U.S. Constitution, federal law is supreme over state laws.[2] So, how can state representatives or citizens of Missouri pass and put into effect a state law that ignores outright bans according to federal law?

Another question that often arises when students of state government discuss the supremacy clause is why there is so much variation in state laws. State and local laws differ in criminal penalties from jay walking to murder. They also differ in other policies that concern abortion, gun regulation, and physician assisted suicide. In order to understand why there are so many differences between states and why Missouri has unique laws of its own one must understand the U.S. federal system. This chapter tackles the question as to how much power states have in creating their own laws. It also covers how Missouri fits into the governmental system as it relates to federal government. From the American Revolution up to our modern times, the ebb and flow of state autonomy in determining its own laws and its relationship to federal power has evolved quite a bit. This chapter covers this evolution and broadly introduces readers to critical stages of state power in the context of Missouri state government.

Unitary, Confederal, and Federal Governmental Systems: A Brief Overview of U.S. Political Development

The relationship between federal government and states has not always been the same. From the time the 13 colonies declared themselves states through the Declaration of Independence to our current modern times, states have gone through variety of phases in their own ability to wield power over the laws of their territories. Missouri was still a western territory occupied by European powers during the inception of the U.S. federal system. However, in order to understand its own power and role with federal government, a brief overview of governmental distribution of power between member units (such as states) is necessary.

American states have their own system of governance, of which all include a legislature, executive (governor's office), and court system. Most states today reflect a similar set-up that had existed during colonial times. This is not surprising because American colonists had experienced a semi-democratic system.[3] Colonial charters allotted these British colonies the ability to create their own laws. A *charter* is a governmental set-up where a higher authority, such as the British King or national parliament, allowed colonies to create their own laws as long as it did not go against laws established by that higher authority. This higher governmental authority also has the power to abolish those laws. Localities, like many American cities today, are dependent on higher government to exist. Because of the geographic distance from Britain, colonies had to set up their own system of governance. One can imagine if the laws of the original American colonies were contingent on the British Crown alone. It could take years for messages to and from Britain to arrive. The American colonies were considered to be semi-democratic because they had some flexibility in creating their own laws. This was done through voting for representatives to create laws in colonial legislatures. Governors were to approve or veto laws that came from colonial legislatures, but, may also have been subject to approval by the British parliament and the Monarch.

As such, the Americans had a long history of many forms of self-governance in a semi-autonomous system. The most significant act of a shift in this power was when the American colonies announced that they were breaking its' ties from Britain and declared themselves states. These new states announced that they had enough power to control their territory as any other autonomous country. A clear delineation of the ties that were broken is written in the 1776 Declaration of Independence:

> *"That these United Colonies are, and of Right ought to be Free and Independent States; that they are Absolved from all Allegiance to the British Crown, and that all political connection between them and the State of Great Britain, is and ought to be totally dissolved; and that as Free and Independent States, they have full Power to levy War, conclude Peace, contract Alliances, establish Commerce, and to do all other Acts and Things which Independent States may of right do."*

These new states, then, reworked their charters to create constitutions and they were no longer subject to a higher governmental authority. They declared the same powers any independent country had such as declaring war, determining an economic system, and entering into alliances.

Breaking political ties with Britain meant treason. As a result, the new American states had to prepare for a forthcoming bloody battle with well-financed super power. In order to fight the war against the British, there needed to be some sort of compact between the new states. Approved by the Continental Congress in 1777 and ratified by the states in 1781, the *Articles of Confederation* helped to create an alliance to fight the war.[4] This is the first confederacy, or *confederal* system, created in U.S. history. It was also the nations' first constitution. A confederacy is where governments enter into a compact with one another. Sovereign powers are not derived from a central government, but from a states' constitution. Under the Articles of Confederation, each state had one vote in Continental Congress. For any agreement to go into effect, a supermajority was necessary—nine out of thirteen states had to vote 'yes'. This is an obvious difference from the charter system the colonies had with Britain.

A confederal system also differs from a *unitary* system of government. A unitary system of government is when all power is vested in national government. It is a centralized system where political sub-units such as cities, counties, and provinces, carry out policy made by national government. In a unitary system, these political sub-units are administrative appendages of national government. Countries that have a unitary system of government include France, Israel, China, and Sweden.

The Articles of Confederation helped these newly formed states to fight the British. They served as a form of an alliance and were in effect from 1777 to 1787. Still, during this time period, what we know now as Missouri resided in the Louisiana Territory occupied by the Spanish. Nevertheless, there were a variety of problems that states began to face under the Articles of Confederation. First, the war was expensive and the states had to pay off accrued debt borrowed from other countries such as France and Holland. It became difficult to pay this debt as the Articles of Confederation did not allow levying of taxes on states. Also, although the articles clearly stated that states could not make treaties with other states and countries, this stipulation was critiqued as unenforceable. This made some leaders uneasy about the stability of the confederal system after the American Revolution.

There were also some problems involving ex-Revolutionary war soldiers. Some soldiers came home from the war to find that they were being heavily taxed—which was an economic burden they could not afford. One defining event that spurred political elites to reconsider the political system under the Articles of Confederation was *Shay's Rebellion*. Upset about hefty land taxes and not receiving back pay for fighting the Revolutionary war, ex-Revolutionary war veterans gathered together under the command of Daniel Shays. Shays army of about 2,000 farmers staged a revolt in Massachusetts. This revolt proved difficult for the Massachusetts Governor to quash and was eventually put down by armies paid for by elites. The inability for the state of Massachusetts to put down this rebellion was a defining moment that cast more light on the weakness of the Articles of Confederation. After this rebellion and with consideration of all the weakness of the confederacy, a Constitutional Convention was called. This began the federal system that the United States has today.

ARTICLES
OF
CONFEDERATION
AND
PERPETUAL UNION
BETWEEN THE
STATES
OF

NEW-HAMPSHIRE, MASSACHUSETTS-BAY, RHODE-ISLAND AND PROVIDENCE PLANTATIONS, CONNECTICUT, NEW-YORK, NEW-JERSEY, PENNSYLVANIA, DELAWARE, MARY-LAND, VIRGINIA, NORTH-CAROLINA, SOUTH-CAROLINA AND GEORGIA.

LANCASTER, (PENNSYLVANIA,) PRINTED:

BOSTON, Re-printed by JOHN GILL, Printer to the GENERAL ASSEMBLY.
M,DCC,LXXVII.

© Everett Historical/Shutterstock.com

Articles of Confederation

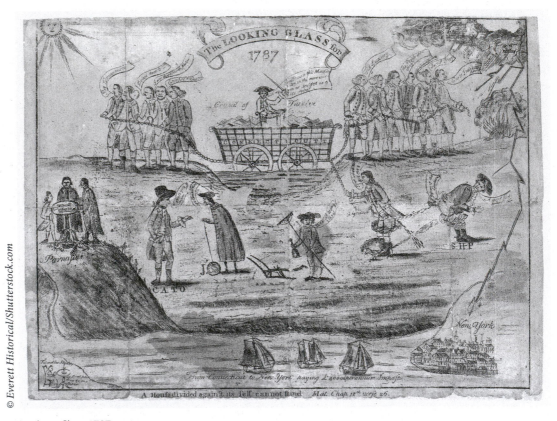

Looking Glass 1787

The Federal System and the Development of the U.S. Constitution

The weakness of the Articles of Confederation led political elites to reconsider the confederal system of government. Although not all of them agreed on how strong central government should be. Disagreement was over how much power states were willing to give up in order to have a much more stable governmental system. It was generally agreed that a federal form of government should be set in place. Federalism or a *federal* form of government is when there is a division of authority between sub national units, which are the states, and a national authority. Unlike a unitary form of government, states are not just the administrative arms of government. States have discrete powers of their own. These powers are derived from the federal constitution and a state's own constitution. Still, this is different from a confederal system in that national government has the last say in what states can do according to the national constitution.

Arguments for or against a federal system pitted on many different views as to how to deal with states maintaining their own autonomy. Arguments for federalism were articulated in the *Federalist Papers* by John Jay, Alexander Hamilton, and James Madison. These papers were meant to get popular support to buy into a federal system. They included simple and complex arguments in favor of the proposed U.S. Constitution. The writers argued that the new system would balance the powers between branches, states, and national government.

Alexander Hamilton, in Federalist Paper number 28 wrote that under this new system, Americans would be able to shift their loyalties back and forth between national and local government. With state representatives in the lower house and U.S. Senate, it would

TABLE 1: Differences between Governmental Systems: Unitary, Confederal, and Federal Government		
Unitary	**Confederal**	**Federal**
All powers are vested in national government. Political Sub-units administer national government policy.	A compact exists between political sub-units but national powers are weak. Political sub-units, such as states, have final say over laws in their territories.	There is a division of power between political sub-units and national government. While political sub-units have autonomy in making laws, they also share power with national government. However, national laws are supreme to state laws.

give states the ability to keep local and national interests in control of one another and enhance liberties at both levels of government.[5] Hamilton argued that it gave the "ability to unite common forces for the protection of common liberties." Overall, the Federalist papers sought to illustrate that the U.S. Constitution would overcome the deficiencies of the Articles of Confederation and granted states a forum of deliberation and ways to agree on issues through a national legislature—U.S. Congress. It granted the ability for states to come together to agree on the power to tax, maintain a national army, and regulate commerce—features not provided in the Articles of Confederation. It also gave broad powers for states to have the ability to govern within their own territories according to their own constitutions.

Probably one of the most grounded arguments that states maintained a significant amount of power and were better off in a federal system was James Madison's arguments in Federalist Papers number 45 and 46. In these papers, Madison argued that states would benefit with the U.S. Constitution because they would receive protection in the form of national security. One can argue that Shay's rebellion highlighted the inability of the state of Massachusetts to quell internal conflict. If an internal conflict could not be handled well, it could be prime time for outside forces to attack a state. For those who were concerned about states losing power in a federal system, Madison also made the point that federal government is in fact dependent on state governments to exist. This argument was made when the U.S. Constitution stipulated that state legislatures voted to elect the U.S. President. A states' state legislature also selected their representative in the U.S. Senate, while U.S. House members are elected by popular vote by citizens of a state. Madison argued that state governments had the advantage because the make-up of federal government is contingent on states to exist. Additionally, Madison argued, the powers given to federal government were few and clear and the power designated to state governments allowed states broad powers to govern over internal affairs.

It is important to point out that many Americans during this time period identified with their states. One may say that they were a 'Virginian' or a 'New Yorker' before they would identify as an American. These states had such vast differences in industry, geography, and culture. In fact, along with the powers these states had during the Articles of Confederation, each state could be a considered small country.[6] It is therefore no surprise how some were resistant to the idea of federalism.

Coming together as a union under a federal system meant giving up some powers. An Anti-federalist under the pen-name of Cato, was concerned about the stability of a federal system. He was concerned about the diversity of interests and differences between states.

How can federal government control states with such dissimilar interests? In an ominous and perhaps foreshadowing statement about the stability of the system based on dissimilar interests, Cato argued against federalism. Cato wrote, "this un-kindred legislature therefore, composed of interests opposite and dissimilar in their nature, will in its exercise, emphatically be, like a house divided against itself."[7] Cato argued that a union would need to be held together by force at the cost of liberty. Thomas Jefferson had the same concerns during the debates on the Missouri Question concerning the issue of slavery. Cato's statement should sound familiar to history buffs. Abraham Lincoln in his 1858 speech while running for U.S. Senate used the same quote when referring to the issue of slavery. In particular, he was referring to the 1854 *Kansas-Nebraska Act* while trying to differentiate himself from his opponents.[8] The Kansas-Nebraska Act divided the land west of Missouri into Kansas and Nebraska, of which those territories would decide whether or not to be pro-slavery or antislavery. This violated the Missouri Compromise and further divided the country over the issue of slavery. In this famous speech, future President Abraham Lincoln may have unwittingly foreshadowed the second confederal system in U.S. history—which occurred during the Civil War.

Powers of National Government and State Governments

Although American history and politics is riddled with issues that involved disagreements and varied interests, the American system has been stable and still stands today as the oldest living democracy in the world. The federalist argument ultimately won when the U.S. Constitution was ratified in 1787, despite Cato's and a number of anti-federalist concerns. Some of the anti-federalist concerns were addressed through the addition of the first ten amendments of the U.S. Constitution in 1791 called the *Bill of Rights*. The body of the U.S. Constitution and the Bill of Rights lists the power of federal government and the powers of state governments.

As discussed in Chapter 2, like the Missouri Constitution and all state constitutions, the U.S. Constitution lays out the powers of federal branches in Article I (U.S. Congress), Article II (Executive), and Article III (Judiciary). Within those Articles of the U.S. Constitution, both federal and states' rights and powers are listed. Many of the powers of national government are described in the first Article of the U.S. Constitution. While Congress, the national legislature can declare war and print money, states are forbidden to do so. Also in the first Article, is the *commerce clause*. The commerce clause gives national government the power to regulate *interstate commerce*, that is, commerce between foreign nations, states, and Indian tribes. Over time, the interstate commerce clause has given U.S. Congress broad powers to regulate the environment, firearms, internet transactions, and even racial segregation. U.S. Congress also has the power to tax imports and exports. States are given the right to regulate *intrastate commerce*—business dealings and transactions within a states' territory.

Article I, section 8 also gives U.S. Congress wide discretion of powers through the *necessary and proper clause*, also known as the 'elastic clause.' The first section of Article I of the U.S. Constitution enumerates, or lists, the powers of Congress. At the end of this list it states that Congress shall have the power to "make all Laws which shall be necessary and proper for carrying into Execution the foregoing Powers...." This means that law making powers of Congress are "elastic" in that it can make laws not listed in order to execute the powers that are already listed.

The Case of the Great Chicken Caper—Scrambling Over Interstate Commerce and Cage Size

Laws created in some states affect other states—especially when it has to do with regulation and commerce. In 2014, California passed a law that required all eggs sold in the state to come from chickens whose cage sizes are twice the size of the chicken industry standards. In order to maintain a foot in the rather large California egg market, many mid-west farmers have to change the size of chicken cages. While the state of California claims that it is well within their right under the intrastate commerce clause to have this law, other states argue that it is an interstate commerce issue. Many egg-producing states, including Missouri, are fighting this new law.

While Articles I through III of the U.S. Constitution define the powers between the branches, it also lists the powers of national government, and denies some powers to states. Article IV of the U.S. Constitution focuses more specifically on states. Article IV section 1 stipulates that states must give *full-faith and credit* to other states. This means that states have to accept other states records and judicial proceedings such as marriage licenses, driver's licenses, and criminal proceedings. For example, if someone from Kansas has a valid Kansas driver's license and drives in Missouri, then the state of Missouri recognizes that they can legally drive. One may ask, though, the reason why some states, such as Missouri, did not recognize same-sex marriage when other states were granting licenses

"States Scramble over Chicken Cage Sizes"

© PavelSvoboda/Shutterstock.com

to same-sex couples. This was an exception. In 1996, Congress passed the Defense of Marriage Act (DOMA) which was signed into law by President Bill Clinton. DOMA was a federal law that stipulated that states do not have to legally recognize same sex marriage and had been interpreted to even denying a grant of divorce.

Article IV, section 2, has what is known as the privileges and immunities clause. The privileges and immunities clause stipulates that states cannot discriminate against citizens of another state. This means that a state, for example, cannot deny a citizen from another state access to the court system or pursuing a profession. If someone wants to pursue litigation in the state of Missouri they cannot deny this option unless the lawsuit is under the jurisdiction of another state. There are some reasonable contingencies, however. In order to vote in the state of Missouri, for example, if one just moved from Arkansas, they must have status as a Missouri resident. Some have argued that out of state tuition prices for college violate the privileges and immunities clause. A college student who is from Florida may have to pay higher price to go to a university in Missouri.

States have the power to regulate commerce and determine other types of regulations.

© Reid Morth/Shutterstock.com

However, this has been considered a beneficial service by the U.S. Supreme Court in which the state has property rights. Higher costs for non-residents also apply to reasonable hikes in prices for fishing and hunting licenses.[9]

What Can States Do?—Plenty

With the denials of powers that the U.S. Constitution places on states, what can states do? There are an abundance of things that states can do as long as it does not violate federal law. In any given year, states create more laws that apply to their jurisdictions than U.S. Congress. This is because they are the first to jump on issues that pertain to the state. States are innovative in creating policies that apply to things such as alternative modes of transportation, paving roads, creating state tax incentives, or changing criminal codes. The federal system allows states to take on projects quickly.

Much of state power is wielded through the *10th Amendment* in the Bill of Rights. The 10th Amendment gives *reserved powers* to states. Reserved powers are defined as powers not given to national government through the Constitution are reserved for the states. This means that if federal law does not exist, then states have the power to create laws as long as it does not violate the U.S. Constitution. For example, a national law banning the death penalty does not exist and this absence allows Missouri to have a death penalty. This allows for states a choice in deciding whether or not to have a death penalty. Unless it violates the U.S. Constitution or it has been ruled by the U.S. Supreme court to violate it, states have a free hand in creating their own laws.

The 10th Amendment is a defining feature of federalism. This allows states such as Missouri much autonomy in creating their own laws and having control in amending the Missouri constitution. The reservation clause illustrates how U.S. states are not just administrative arms of national government such as in a unitary system. However, if national government bans a policy such as the death penalty, then states like Missouri can no longer have it. This is called *federal preemption*—where national government overrides state laws. Federal preemption would not occur in a confederal system, where there is much more autonomy in a political sub-unit's jurisdiction over the laws of its territory.

Missouri, along with other states have other broad powers that constitute a variety of state functions. For example, states have jurisdiction over setting up elections. Article VIII of the Missouri Constitution outlines when elections are to take place as well as residency requirements for voter registration. States can also vary in deciding which years they hold statewide elections. They can also decide how far from an election a citizen must register to vote. While some states have same day registration, Missouri requires someone to register by the 4th Wednesday before an election to qualify to vote. Other state functions include jurisdiction over setting up an educational system and Article IX of the Missouri Constitution sets up the Missouri state Department of Elementary and Secondary Education. It also outlines how much of the Missouri state budget is supposed to go to education. This article of the Missouri Constitution also includes measures to support public libraries.

The Missouri Constitution also defines the powers of local governments such as cities, counties, towns, and villages. Local governments are limited by what states allow them to do. This is known as *Dillon's rule*. Dillon's rule is a legal interpretation that argues that local governments such as towns, cities, and counties are limited by what states say they can do. The idea is that these local jurisdictions are created by states, so that the states have the power to limit or to give the discretion to local government. Article VI of the

RESERVED POWERS
_____

TENTH AMENDMENT

The powers not delegated to the United States by the Constitution, nor prohibited by it to the States, are reserved to the States respectively, or to the people.

Missouri Constitution defines the powers of local governments in the state based on their population size and income. This means that larger cities may have a city council and/or mayor or city manager, while smaller towns with small populations may be under the jurisdiction of the county. The Missouri Constitution gives much of the decision making power over how autonomous local governments are allowed to be to the Missouri state legislature. This feature is common in other states.

Did you know?...

Michigan Takes Over Detroit

The city of Detroit faced a major financial crisis when the 2008 recession hit. In part, because consumers were not buying cars and due to the city's large car manufacturing industry the city was no longer taking in money for government functions. The state of Illinois ended up dissolving city until it can function on its' own.

The 10th Amendment allows for flexibility in creating laws and policy to deal with the wants and needs of states. However, it is important to note that states, including Missouri, are restricted to the parameters of the U.S. Constitution. Even though each state has a Bill of Rights, the fundamental restriction on state governments is the *14th Amendment* of the U.S. Constitution. Section 1 of the 14th Amendment stipulates that all states must give equal protection and due process rights to American citizens. This means that the U.S. Bill of Rights applies to citizens of all states. However, this was not always the case. The following section outlines various periods of federalism—where state and federal power over state actions and citizens varied quite a bit:

Section 1. 14th Amendment:

> *"All persons born or naturalized in the United States, and subject to the jurisdiction thereof, are citizens of the United States and of the state wherein they reside. No state shall make or enforce any law which shall abridge the privileges or immunities of citizens of the United States; nor shall any state deprive any person of life, liberty, or property, without due process of law; nor deny to any person within its jurisdiction the equal protection of the laws."*

Federalism and Missouri—The Changing Relationship Between States and Federal Government

The U.S. Constitution provided a natural tension between national government and state power through denials of state power and the 10th Amendment. However, jurisdiction over certain state and federal powers has shifted since the ratification of the U.S. Constitution in 1787. The era from 1787 through 1865 had few disputes of power between states and federal government. This is mainly because states had historically had autonomy in governance under their own constitutions.

The first challenge to federal power was the case McCulloch v. Maryland in 1819 when the U.S. Supreme court ruled that national government is supreme to the states under the Supremacy Clause of the U.S. Constitution. Still, during this period, states were generally free from national government and this era is characterized by a period of *dual federalism.*

TABLE 2: State Powers

What can states do?	What cannot states do?
Regulate intrastate commerce	Override national law
Conduct elections	Raise armies
Provide for the health and welfare of citizens	Coin money
Create own judiciary	Wage war
Tax state citizens	Deny Full-Faith and Credit
Ratify the U.S. Constitution	Tax federal government
Make and enforce laws	Discriminate against citizens of other states (Privileges and immunities clause)
Create, empower, dissolve, and regulate local government systems	Ignore the Bill of Rights (14th Amendment)

*States can do as they please as long as they do not violate federal law or the U.S. Constitution

Dual federalism is a precise separation of national and state authority. From 1787 through 1865, citizens were not protected by the national constitution from a state action—they were under the jurisdiction of a state's constitution in that state. In essence, one can think of citizens being governed by two distinct legal bodies—federal government and state government. In fact, the 1833 U.S. Supreme court ruling *Barron v. Baltimore* reinforced this idea. The U.S. Supreme court ruled that the U.S. Bill of Rights was only applicable to federal action against a citizen and only a state's constitution applied to state actions. This ruling reinforced the idea of a precise zone of power between federal and state government.

Of major concern over these rights was the issue of slavery. The Missouri Compromise in 1820 shook the idea that states could establish power over the people who reside in their states. The question over the Missouri Compromise was whether the federal establishment of slave states and non-slave states was a violation of the states' rights. Many southerners argued that it was. Debate over the Missouri Compromise sparked heated discussion as to what level of government, state or federal government, should have power over the issue of slavery.

The fight over state's rights in the early period of federalism stemmed over the right for states to maintain the institution of slavery if they pleased. It was also born out of economic rights over tariffs imposed on imports. In 1824 Congress passed tariffs which protected northern manufacturing industries and shrunk the demand for southern goods such as cotton. Many from southern states saw these tariffs as favoring the economic status of northern states. In disagreement with the general will of U.S. Congress over tariffs and the Missouri Compromise, southern states grew increasingly uneasy about the power of federal government. In 1828, South Carolinian John C. Calhoun, then U.S. Vice President, proposed an alternative understanding of federal power in relation to states called the *doctrine of nullification*.[10] The doctrine of nullification was the argument that favored the idea that since states created the U.S. Constitution, states would have the right to nullify national law. When U.S. Congress reduced the disagreed upon tariffs southern states backed down on a formal nullification argument. However, this discord did illustrate the intense sectionalism that was rapidly occurring between southerners and northerners.

The debate over states' rights certainly did not end with the reduction of tariffs. Two significant events reignited and hardened the tension between northern and southern states. First, the 1854 Kansas-Nebraska Act divided the land west of Missouri into Kansas and Nebraska, of which those territories would decide whether or not to be pro-slavery or antislavery. The Kansas Nebraska Act violated the Missouri Compromise made 34 years earlier. Meanwhile, a slave named Dred Scott was fighting a legal battle for his freedom in Missouri. Not long after the 1854 Kansas-Nebraska Act, in 1857 the U.S. Supreme court in Dred Scott v. Sanford ruled that slaves and persons of African descent could not become U.S. citizens. This decision, along with the Kansas-Nebraska Act nullified the Missouri Compromise. Upon the election of an anti-slavery Republican Party Presidential candidate, Abraham Lincoln, the ultimate battle over what states can do in their own jurisdictions exploded. The pressure of these issues resulted in the Civil War. Southern states formed a confederacy and tried to secede from the union.

Second Phase of Dual Federalism: 1865–1932

The issue of slavery and the Civil War was the ultimate battle over a federal system of government. Split in support, Missouri actually had two state governments whose representatives were sent to U.S. Congress and the Confederacy. The Civil War ended in 1865 with the Union clinging to victory. The outcome was a shift in power over the jurisdiction of citizens. This is when the second short-lived Missouri Constitution was adopted. This constitution, which abolished slavery provisions and was the well-known "Drake Constitution" as discussed in Chapter 2, was Draconian in nature.[11] During this period the Civil War Amendments were added to the U.S. Constitution and included the 13th, 14th, and 15th Amendments. The 13th Amendment freed the slaves. The 15th Amendment gave the right to vote to all men who were U.S. citizens. The amendment that changed the relationship between citizens and states and has been widely used for many civil rights cases is the 14th Amendment. Recall, the 14th Amendment gives all persons equal protection and due process under the law. This means that states now had to abide by the national Bill of Rights and not just their own constitutions. Although this period from 1865 through 1932 is still considered dual federalism, where there are distinct zones of powers between national and federal government, this was a significant shift in power over citizens' rights. Citizens had protections against state action if states violated the federal Bill of Rights. The Civil War settled the dispute of any question that states had to accept national authority. The 14th Amendment cemented it.

Cooperative Federalism— New Responsibilities for States

Often political systems change during some sort of crisis. The crisis over the issue of states' rights over slavery ended with a series of amendments to the U.S. Constitution that changed the relationship between citizens and state governments. The next crisis that altered the relationship between states and federal government can be linked to industrialization and the Great Depression. During the 1870s through the early 1900s the American economy became increasingly complex. Urbanization, high immigration to urban areas, and industrialization altered the living situation of many Americans. A variety of different issues began to emerge. Industrialization led to poor working conditions with a lack of labor laws. This was a period of time when it was not expected that federal government would step in to take care of issues involving the relationship between businesses and employees. Further, cities and other localities were growing and in need of tackling issues of basic services such as sewer, clean water, and trash services.

In order to move on infrastructure such as sanitation, localities would have to ask state government for permission. The third Missouri Constitution ratified in 1875 was during a period of high immigration and adapted to the issue of urbanization and growth. The 1875 constitution allowed for large local governments such as St. Louis to have more say in how to address needs through "home-rule." Home-rule allotted more autonomy in providing governmental services.[12] Many states began to adopt these types of measures to adjust to the changing social and business environment. However, a looming shock to the system was about to occur when Americans faced the deepest depression in U.S. history—the Great Depression in the 1930s. The Great Depression was a crisis that again, changed the relationship between federal government and state government.

The Great Depression began after the stock market crashed in 1929. Panicked, many citizens made a run on the banks where they pulled out all of their money. Some citizens never recovered their funds from banks because the banks ran out of money—and insurance on funds in banks did not exist. Unemployment was as high as 23% nationally and sometimes higher in urban areas such as St. Louis, Missouri.[13] It did not help that farmers in the Midwest, including Missouri, faced a drought which caused a massive dust-bowl resulting in failed crops. The United States was in a massive economic disaster. This period of time, federal government was not expected to step in to provide services to citizens or help to bail out businesses to jump start the economy. Assistance that we know of today, did not exist. Food stamps, temporary financial aid, social security, medical aid, etc., was not provided by government. Americans were on their own, with states at their financial wits end.

In 1932, Presidential candidate, Franklin Delano Roosevelt (FDR), campaigned on recovery from the depression through the New Deal. The New Deal was a series of legislation that ended up transforming national governments' responsibilities towards citizens and its' relationship with the states. FDR won a landslide victory for the Presidential seat in 1932. During his tenure as president, much of the New Deal legislation that he pushed, passed into law. The result was a variety of measures to help those in need of financial support as well as provision of government funded jobs. These measures were meant to stimulate the economy and not just subsidize those out of work. Changes included unemployment insurance, social security, Aid to Families with Dependent Children (AFDC), subsidies to

farmers, as well as the development of the Works Progress Administration and Civilian Conservation Corp, to name a few. Why would these new government programs change the relationship between citizens, states, and federal government? This was the beginning of a period in which states would share responsibilities with federal government to administer these programs—called *cooperative federalism*. Cooperative federalism is where the lines of state and national zones of power and responsibilities and not narrowly defined. There is cooperation and shared responsibilities between federal and state governments in administering programs—a big difference from discrete zones of power between federal, state, and local government.

Other events that expanded the role of federal government in relation to citizens and states were World War II, and President Lindon B. Johnson's Great Society programs. World War II dramatically increased the size of the federal bureaucracy. It also

St. Louis

Tea Party Political Rally in St. Louis

produced subsidies such as veterans' benefits and programs for WWII veterans, as well as federally backed loans to purchase homes. In the 1960s President Johnsons Great Society program included funds for Head Start (pre-kindergarten education for children) and food stamps. Medicare (medical assistance for the elderly) and Medicaid (medical assistance for the poor) were also joint programs administered by federal government with the help of states.

How does federal government get states to administer programs? These programs were administered through federal *categorical grants* and *block grants*. Categorical grants are aid from federal government to states that are supposed to go to a specific program. A categorical grant for Medicare may define a specific area in which these funds must go—such as promoting health checks for diabetes. Block grants are aid to states from federal government that are supposed to go to a specific issue, but, states have more discretion as to how to use the funds. A block grant from federal government for homeland security may mean a state can funnel those funds to a variety of areas such as new fire personnel or fire trucks, or software programs to monitor drones.

Since the 1970s there has been some backlash over the battle of power for a states' right to choose how to administer federally funded programs—or at least have some discretion as to the guidelines of those programs. Much of this discussion took place in the 1980s during Ronald Reagans Presidency. President Reagan campaigned on and argued to reduce welfare and 'decentralize' power back to the states. The idea was to devolve the responsibility and autonomy over these programs to the states to give them a choice in how to administer these programs—however this big shift was rejected by Congress. Although welfare funds were reduced during his Presidency, states started to use more of their own funds to continue the programs.

Ronald Reagan reignited the debate over states' rights, mirroring John C. Calhoun's rhetoric of nullification. In his inaugural address, Reagan stated that "All of us need to be reminded that Federal Government did not create the States; the States created Federal Government."[14] States' rights advocates have more recently emerged and revived this debate. Some, though, would like to have states right advocates take a step back when thinking about Reagan's states right argument. Political scientist David Webber, cautions citizens and writes that when President Reagan said "that the 13 colonies created the federal government, not the other way around," ..."he is right—but the federal government created, or purchased, most of the other 37 states."[15]

Reagan certainly reinvigorated an ever increasing states' rights movement that we continue to see today. Missouri is not insulated from this as many Missouri state lawmakers are seeking to challenge federal programs and exert the power of the state through the 10th Amendment. This is a conservative movement with a states' right argument to reduce government spending and regain ground in other areas such as abortion and gun rights. The 2013 Missouri legislative session passed a law that nullifies federal gun laws. Although this law was vetoed by Governor Jay Nixon, it is symbolic in that the states' rights movement is alive and well in the Missouri legislature. Resistance of Missouri lawmakers to implement the federal Affordable Care Act is another example. However, still many Missourians are concerned about reduction in federal benefits that are distributed through and supplemented by the state. There is certain back and forth debate over particular features of cooperative federalism in the state. Even though Medicaid expansion, for example, was supported by many citizens in the state of Missouri in 2015, it was rejected by the Missouri state legislature.

★ Conclusion

The relationship between states and federal government has changed significantly over time. Under dual federalism, prior to the Civil War, citizens were ruled by two distinct zone of power—federal government and state government. During that period of time, states enjoyed relative autonomy in laws and governance. However, with the insidious issue of slavery, the strength and stability of the federal system was placed under the ultimate litmus test through the Civil War. The 14th Amendment changed the relationship between the states, their citizens, and federal government. A second dramatic change began due to the Great Depression and FDR's New Deal policies. From then on, states have had a much more intricate relationship with federal government by cooperating in administering federally funded programs.

Despite the debate over states' rights, states have a lot of leeway in governing over their jurisdictions. States have the right to do plenty in their states. Despite denials of power in full-faith and credit, the privileges and immunities clause, and other stipulations as laid out in the U.S. Constitution, the 10th Amendment allots states much power. States can set up their own judicial system, figure out ways to pave their own roads, set up school systems, control local government, tax and spend, make changes to their own constitutions, and much more. Missouri's Constitution provides this framework for the state. Articles VI through XII of the Missouri Constitution address how the state is to handle everything from education, railroads, and elections.

Political scientist Daniel Elazar described the political culture of United States as a mosaic.[16] The United States is quite geographically large, and although Americans may have different interests and come from different political cultures, federalism certainly helps hold the states together with a certain amount of state autonomy. Another feature of federalism is the flexibility in which states can experiment with policy. Because states can do much within their own jurisdictions, the American political system has often been described as "laboratories of democracy," a term coined by Justice Louis Brandies. In a 1932 court decision Brandies wrote "It is one of the happy incidents of the federal system that a single courageous State may, if its citizens choose, serve as a laboratory; and try novel social and economic experiments without risk to the rest of the country."[17] Missouri certainly enjoys this status as a state as it has amended its Constitution and experimented with policy to serve as a laboratory of democracy.

★ KEY TERMS ★

Supremacy Clause	Kansas-Nebraska Act	Dillon's Rule
Charter	Commerce Clause	14th Amendment
Articles of Confederation	Interstate Commerce	Dual Federalism
Confederal	Intrastate Commerce	Barron v. Baltimore
Federal	Necessary and Proper Clause	Doctrine of Nullification
Unitary	Full-Faith and Credit	Cooperative Federalism
Shay's Rebellion	10th Amendment	Categorical Grants
Bill of Rights	Reserved Powers	Block Grants
Federalist Papers	Federal Preemption	

★ ENDNOTES ★

1   Missouri v. Robinson (2015)

2   See McCulloch v. Maryland 1819.

3   Squire, Peverill and Keith E. Hamm. 2005. 101 Chambers: Congress, State Legislatures, and the Future of Legislative Studies. The Ohio State University Press: Columbus.

4   A Century of Lawmaking for a New Nation: U.S. Congressional Documents and Debates, 1774–1875. *Journals of the Continental Congress,* Volume 9.

5   Hamilton, alexander, James Madison, and John Jay. The Federalist Papers. 2003. Bantam Dell: New York.

6   McLaughlin, Andrew C. "The Confederdation and the Constitution" in *A History of the American Nation.* Ed. Albert Bushnell Hart. 1905. Harper and Brothers: New York.

7   Cato's Letters No. 3. The Founders' Constitution Volume 1, Chapter 4, Document 16. The University of Chicago Press. Available at http://press-pubs.uchicago.edu/founders/documents/v1ch4s16.html

8   See Fehrenbacher, Don E. 1960. "The Origins and Purpose of Lincolns "House Divided" Speech. *The Mississippi Valley Historical Review* 46(4): 615–643.

9   Although these cannot be unreasonable in which states overwhelmingly favor their own citizens.

10 *The Papers of John C. Calhoun, vol. 10, 1825–1829.* Columbia: University of South Carolina Press. 1977.

11 March, David D. "Drake Charles Daniel (1811–1892)" in *Dictionary of Missouri Biography.* 1999. EdsLawerence O. Christensen, William E. Foley, Gary R. Kremer, and Kenneth H. Winn.

12 Swindler, William F. 1958. Missouri's Constitutions: History, Theory, and Practice. William and Mary Law School. *Faculty Publications.* Paper 1618. http://scholarship.law.wm.edu/facpubs/1618

13 See Margo, Robert A. Employment and Unemployment in the 1930s. Journal of Economic Perspectives, 7(2): 41–59.

14 Ronald Reagan: "Inaugural Address," January 20, 1981. Online by Gerhard Peters and John T. Woolley, *The American Presidency Project.* http://www.presidency.ucsb.edu/ws/?pid=43130.

[15] Webber, David. "State Sovereignty and the F-Word." The Missouri Record, January 19th, 2010. Available at: http://www.missourirecord.com/news/index.asp?article=10086

[16] Elazar, Daniel. "The American Mosiac."

[17] New State Ice Co. v. Liebman (1932)

Chapter 4

★ Introduction

The last days of the 2015 legislative session was historically tumultuous for the Missouri General Assembly. A variety of legislation was poised for floor votes in both the house and the senate. The General Assembly had taken up issues such as voter ID laws, right to work legislation, and the use of deadly force in response to issues in Ferguson. Both chambers were fighting to pass or stalwart legislation. On the second to last day of the legislative session, Senate Democrats were busy trying to stop a right to work bill and to open debate on medic-aid expansion. The house was also hustling to get scheduled legislation voted on before the session closed. Meanwhile, Senate Republicans who were the majority party imposed a rare rule to force votes, overriding floor debate. This set up wall of defeat for democrats. But, attention soon was turned to a last minute scandal at the statehouse over relations between then House Speaker John Diehl and a college intern. Reporters converged on Speaker Diehl and he resigned the

Missouri State Capitol Building

© Nagel Photography/Shutterstock.com

next day. This made the Missouri Republican party move on electing a new House Speaker in the midst of an already chaotic end of the session. While house legislators were at a near standstill, Senate Republicans were successful with their initiatives and retained favored legislation by a strategic use of rules. Indeed, these last few days were characterized by a stormy path of strategy and negotiations.

The end of the Missouri legislative session is always very busy. It is the culmination of the hard work legislators have endured over the legislative session. Representatives and Senators have been working on bills for months. They have been conducting hearings, bargaining with each other, finalizing language in bills, and assessing coalitions. These members work hard at pitching bills they would like to see pass before the end of session. The last two weeks are pertinent as the assembly poises to vote on bills that have gone through a five

The End of the Missouri Legislative Session 2015

month process to get to this point. Why are members so eager to get these passed in the final moments of the legislative session? Different from U.S. Congress, the bills worked on in the Missouri General Assembly die at the end of the session, and members have to work from scratch if they are not passed or get out of committee. In U.S. Congress, bills can stay in committee for years and can be referred back for further work.

There are 51 legislative assemblies in the United States—50 state legislatures along with U.S. Congress. All 51 are different from one another, yet, have many similarities. The similarities are due to constructing state constitutions based on the original constitutions of the first 13 states.[1] Differences have much to do with needs within the states, political personalities, and popular opinion. Legislatures morph over time for a variety of reasons. The purpose of this chapter is to give a brief overview of the differences and the similarities between the Missouri General Assembly and U.S. Congress. This chapter will introduce students of Missouri politics to key differences and similarities of the Missouri legislature and U.S. Congress in demographic make-up, party affiliation, resources, lawmaking, and legislative design.

Missouri Legislators, U.S Congressional Members, and Representation: Who Are They?

The United States was built upon the concept of self-governance. The legislative branch is the epitome of a self-governing system where individuals are voted in by citizens to represent particular geographic areas in which they reside. These geographic areas are called **districts**. This type of system is often referred to as a republican form of democracy, or a representative democracy—a step away from direct democracy, where citizens directly vote on legislation. As discussed in earlier chapters, direct democracy exists in Missouri and 23 other states in some form or another. However, much more lawmaking is taken on by individuals who were voted in to represent districts at the state and national levels. U.S. Congress and the Missouri General Assembly have *single member districts*. Single member districts are districts in which one person is elected to the sole seat that exists in the district. *Multimember districts* also exist in the American states. These are districts where there are multiple seats in one district. This means that two, or in some cases, seven individuals can represent one district. Ten states use this system, although Missouri is not one of them.[2]

One question that often arises is whether or not the individuals elected to these positions adequately represent their districts. Representation can take on many different forms, and party affiliation is one of them. The party affiliation of the Missouri state legislature does not reflect the partisan orientation of U.S. Congress. In 2015, 56% of U.S. Congressional members were Republican and 44% were Democrat. While Missouri is known as a fairly moderate state among its partners in the Bible Belt, Republicans certainly weld power in the Missouri legislature. In 2015, 72% of Missouri's legislators were Republican. Most of the minority party democrats come from more urban areas in the state such as Kansas City and St. Louis. With Missouri primarily being a conservative state, it certainly makes sense that its' citizens have voted in so many republicans.

© Christos Georghiou/Shutterstock.com

"Republicans dominate in Missouri legislature which reflects the general public opinion of Missouri citizens."

Another issue of representation is the historically low numbers of women and minorities that have held elective office. Overall, state legislatures have a history of better reflecting citizen demographics than U.S. Congress. However, U.S. Congress is beginning a trend upward in catching up to the overall demographics of race and gender that exists in state legislatures. In 2015, women made up 19.4% of the national legislature and 24.2% of state legislatures.[3] The 2015 Missouri General Assembly ranked in the middle of all states with 24.4% women serving as legislators. As for race, African Americans make up about 12% of the total population. Yet, in 2015 they made up 5.8% of Congress, 9% in state legislatures, and 10% of the Missouri General Assembly.[4] Hispanics are the most underrepresented racial group as they made up 17% of the U.S. population in 2015 but only 5.8% of U.S. Congress, 4% of state legislatures, and 1% of the Missouri state legislature.[5]

Did you know?...

Firsts of the Missouri General Assembly

Did you know that many of the first representatives from Missouri were originally from other states such as Kentucky and West Virginia? It was not until 1960 that Theodore McNeal of St. Louis, was elected as Missouri's first African American state senator. The first white woman elected to the Missouri legislature was Mary Grant in 1972 and the first African American woman Gwen Giles was elected to the state senate in 1977.

Even though state legislatures and U.S. Congress do not reflect population demographics, a substantial upward trend has occurred since the 1970s.[6] While looking at these numbers, one should note that states differ quite a bit in racial make-up. They also differ in political cultures, and electoral systems. For example, states that have moralistic political cultures tend to have more women in their state legislature.[7] States with higher percentages of racial

TABLE 1:	2015 Comparative Demographic Make-up of U.S. Congress, U.S. State Legislatures, and the Missouri General Assembly		
	Women	African Americans	Hispanics
U.S. Congress	19.4%	5.8%	5.8%
State Legislatures	24.2%	9%	4%
Top Three States	Vermont: 41.1% Colorado: 41% Arizona: 35.6%	Mississippi: 29% Alabama: 25% Maryland: 23%	New Mexico: 44% California: 23% Texas: 20%
Bottom Three States	Louisiana: 11.8% Oklahoma: 12.8% Wyoming: 13.3%	HI, ID, IA, ME, MT, NH, ND, SD, UT, and WI have no African Americans in their state legislatures.	AL, AK, AR, HI, IA, KY, LA, ME, MS, NE, NH, ND, OH, PA, SC, SD, VT, and WV, do not have any Hispanics in their state legislatures.
Missouri	24.4%	10%	1%

Cite From Congressional Quarterly, NCSL, and Center for Women and Politics

minorities also have more African Americans, Hispanics, and Asians in their legislatures. Still, the highest and lowest values for race and gender in state legislatures, by far, defeat representation reflected in U.S. Congress (see Table 1). For both state legislatures and U.S. Congress, the most common demographic for representatives across the board are older white males. As for job experience, the most common occupations are in law and business.[8]

A point of discussion that arises when it comes to the race and gender of representatives is whether or not it matters. Are *constituents*, the people that elected officials represent, better served if the representative reflects their race and/or gender? A variety of studies illustrate that African Americans and women do tend to push for legislation that reflects their groups' interests.[9] Research also shows that outputs of state legislatures reflect the public opinions of its' citizens very well.[10] However, research also exists that illustrates that white men who represent districts of color also substantially represent constituent policy preferences quite well.[11]

Another question that arises is whether or not the representative should always vote according to popular opinion of their districts, or as someone who is entrusted to vote their conscious—even if it goes against the grain of popular opinion. A representative who pursues legislation and votes according to the popular opinion of their district is considered to be a *delegate*. A *trustee* is a representative who may not pursue policy or vote according to the popular opinion of their district. This is because it is assumed that the trustee may have more information about the matter or votes according to their own conscious about the issue. One must keep in mind that as issues have become increasingly complex, it is very difficult for representatives to please everyone in their districts.

Qualifying for Office

Race and gender are not criteria for election to state or U.S. legislatures. However, there are differences in age requirements to gain elective office for both U.S. Congress and the Missouri General Assembly. The Missouri General Assembly is similar to the U.S. legislature in that there are two chambers—the house and the senate. The house is commonly referred to the *lower chamber* and the senate, the *upper chamber*. All but one state has two chambers in its state legislature. Nebraska is the only state in the union that has a unicameral legislature. The Missouri Constitution lays out the powers of the two chambers as well as the qualifications for serving as a member. Article I of the U.S. Constitution requires House members to be 25-years-old and a U.S. citizen for seven years. U.S. Senate Members must be 30-years-old and a U.S. citizen for at least nine years. For both positions, members must live in the state and respective district they represent. Article III of the Missouri Constitution defines the qualifications for serving in the General Assembly. A house member must be 24-years-old and a senate member 30. In order to qualify to represent a district, individuals must be a qualified voter for two years in Missouri and have at least one year of residency in the district they will represent.

A noticeable similarity between the requirements of serving in the national legislature and Missouri's legislature is that members of the Senate must be older in order to qualify to hold a seat. This requirement was discussed during the Constitutional Convention. The logic is laid out in founding father James Madison's Federalist Paper number 62. The upper chamber was meant to have members who were more mature and deliberate when making policy. The nature of the U.S. Senate, and state senates alike, does give credence to this general rule. Senates are much more deliberative bodies than the lower chambers where some of the younger members are still navigating the legislative process. Many senators have astute political experience, and they have climbed the political ladder by serving in the lower house before serving in the senate. When asked at a university event about the difference between the Missouri House and Senate, one Missouri State Senator noted that some of the legislation that comes from house are underdeveloped or can be just plain silly. Referring to the types of bills that originate in the house, the Senator stated 'all of the nuts roll over from the house' and 'the senate is the one that cracks them.'[12]

Did you know?...

At Conception or Birth? Defining Missouri's Age Requirement for Elective Office

In 1990, John Stiles filed for candidacy to run for election to the Missouri House of Representatives. Then Secretary of State Roy Blunt denied his application because Stiles would not be 24 years old at the time of service if he won the race. In fact, he would be 23½ years old by the time he would have been sworn into office. Stiles sued stating that it violated the equal protection clause of the 14th Amendment of the U.S. Constitution. Also citing a Missouri statute that life begins at conception, he argued that he met the age requirement according to that definition. The courts decided that "the age requirement rationally furthers the state's legitimate interest in ensuring mature and experienced legislators…" and that "age should be calculated from his date of birth, rather than his date of conception."[13]

Membership Size and District Population

One of the most apparent differences between the Missouri General Assembly and U.S. Congress are in membership size. U.S. Congress has 535 members with 435 representatives in the house and 100 Senators in the senate. Since each state gets two Senators in the national legislature, Missouri has two national senators. The U.S. house is apportioned by population size and Missouri has 8 representatives. Meanwhile, the Missouri legislature has a total of 197 members with 163 house representatives and 34 state senators. One thing in common, which is the norm in all states is that the senate remains exclusive with a smaller number

© Nagel Photography/Shutterstock.com

Missouri House of Representatives

of seats. U.S. Senate districts constitute states. This means that especially in largely populated states, senators represent more people. All states vary in the size of their legislature and are not related to the states' population.[14] The state of New Hampshire, for example, has 400 seats in its' legislature. This is the largest legislature according to the size of the states' eligible voters. Meanwhile, California, has only 120 members in its' state legislature.

As of 2015, Missouri house members represent about 37,000 individuals, while Missouri State Senators represent about 178,340 individuals. Members of the U.S. House of Representatives have about 733,000 individuals in any given district. This varies by state for U.S. Senators because each state is allotted two Senators and vary in population size. Some states and areas in states gain and lose population for a variety of reasons. Shifts in populations may be due to job opportunities or cultural trends. The U.S. political system adapts to these change. In fact, Article III of the Missouri Constitution sets out the guidelines for adjusting districts based on population called *redistricting*. Redistricting is the redrawing of district lines and occurs every 10 years. Redistricting takes place after the U.S. Census provides estimates the population. The census is required by Article 1, section 2 of the U.S. Constitution.

The U.S. Supreme Court has ruled that districts cannot be malapportioned. *Malapportionment* of districts is a scenario when one district has many more individuals than another district. For example, if district A has 1,000 individuals in it and district B has 10,000 individuals, these districts are malapportioned. The Supreme Court ruled in the 1962 *Baker v. Carr* court case that malapportionment violated the 'one person, one vote' principle. So, all districts for federal office in the U.S House of Representatives had to be drawn with equal populations. Only a few years later, in the 1964 court case Reynolds v. Simms this principle of redistricting was applied to state redistricting procedures.

To view the Missouri General Assemblies' House and Senate districts go to: https://ogi. oa.mo.gov/LEGIS/legislativeDistrict/index.html

Terms of Service

Like U.S. House members, Missouri house members serve two year terms. U.S. Senators serve six year terms and Missouri state senators have four year terms. Terms of service in the Missouri General Assembly are limited but are not for members of U.S. Congress. *Term limits* began with a populist revolt in the early 1990s against *incumbents*. Incumbents are individuals who are the current holders of elective office. The concern was that since incumbents are often difficult to unseat, there was an uneven distribution of power in state legislatures. Some were concerned that these politicians were entrenched with interest groups and because it was difficult to win against them in an election, they may not be serving the interests of their districts. The idea was to get 'fresh blood' into these seats and have the ability to unseat politicians without having to hold an election. In 1992, the citizens of Missouri voted to pass a constitutional amendment to limit the number of terms legislators could serve. Since then, there has been an eight year limit for both the house and the senate. This means that legislators can serve a total of 16 years in the Missouri Assembly, but after that they are banned for life from running for office in the Missouri legislature again.[15] U.S. Congress does not have a limit on the number of terms individuals can serve in office.

TABLE 2: Missouri General Assembly and US Congress: Requirements, Size, and Office Professionalism

	Missouri General Assembly	U.S. Congress
Age Requirement	House: 24 Senate: 30	House: 25 Senate: 30
Size	House: 163 Senate: 34	House: 435 Senate: 100
Terms of Service	House: 2 years Senate: 4 years Term limits: Two 8 year terms	House: 2 years Senate: 6 years Term limits: None
Legislative Professionalism	Length of Session: January through May Salary: $35,915 Paid Staff: Yes	Length of Session: Year around Salary: $174,000 Paid Staff: Yes

Office Resources

Legislatures are different and similar in many ways. This also includes what scholars have described as *legislative professionalism*.[16] Professionalism for legislatures is based on days in session, legislator salary, and staff size. The measurement is based on U.S. Congress as being the most professionalized office which is in session year around and has the highest paid staff and resources. Rank and file members of the national legislature get paid about $174,000 a year and have full-time staff to help their offices function. The Missouri General Assembly is in session five months out of the year from the beginning of January to the end of May. Generally, members come to the state Capitol in Jefferson City to work from Monday through Thursday, then go to their home districts and start the week over again on Monday. As of 2015, Missouri state legislators are paid a salary of $35,915 a year.[17] Compared to other legislatures, the Missouri General Assembly has a sizable staff. In 2009 the National Conference of State Legislatures counted 474 permanent staff members in the Missouri General Assembly.[18] The Missouri state legislature ranks in the middle and is considered to be semi-professional, or a *part-time legislature*. Other state legislatures may only be in session 30 days out of the year and have half the salary of Missouri's. States that have more professionalized legislatures are usually states that have complex economies and diverse social systems. This makes sense since these states have a diversity of issues it needs to deal with. Diverse issues put pressure on the legislature, and as a result, may require longer sessions. These states include California, Illinois, and New York. The least professionalized legislatures, often called *citizen-legislatures*, are Arkansas, New Hampshire, and Wyoming.[19] Compared to the U.S. Congress, the Missouri legislature is larger in size, less professionalized, and term limited, but it has very similar age requirements (see Table 2).

Lawmaking and Legislative Design:
Key Differences in How a Bill Becomes a Law

The process of how a bill becomes a law is not necessarily in the U.S. Constitution or the Missouri Constitution. Both Constitutions give power to the legislature to create laws, but, its process is largely left up to members. Members create house and senate rules, which are mainly created by the political party that has majority status in the chamber. However, there are certain stipulations placed on members actions according to the U.S and Missouri Constitutions. With rules, personalities of leaders, and Constitutional limitations, how a bill becomes a law can be very complex. The process can be so complex that it could theoretically take volumes of books to explain. However, describing the overall process in simple form is in fact, feasible. The purpose of this section is to make a basic comparison of the Missouri legislative process to the legislative process of U.S. Congress. Here, the introduction of bills, committee systems, and basic differences in rules will be discussed. The complexity of the system can certainly lead one to point to Prussian politician Otto von Bismark's description of the legislative process—"laws are like sausages, it is better off not to see them be made." Without getting our hands too dirty in the lawmaking process, the following is a clean attempt at explaining it as neatly as possible.

Introducing a Bill

U.S. Congress and the Missouri state legislature actually had similar procedures in how a bill becomes law. This holds true more so in the early 1820s than today. Divergence from similarity is due to inside and outside pressures on the legislative branch. This could be from changing economic and political environments, to just plain strong personalities. This is also exasperated through a changing partisan system. Of course, office professionalism (length of session, resources, and staff) contributes to differences in the lawmaking process and policy outputs. Many factors affect how a bill, otherwise known as legislation, becomes a law for the 50 state legislatures as well as the national legislature.

1: Drafting Legislation

How a bill becomes a law begins with drafting legislation. Drafting legislation simply means that legislation is written. Bills have to be introduced to the assembly by a sitting representative in both U.S. Congress and the Missouri General Assembly. However, it can be drafted by anyone. This process allows for citizens and the executive branch to present their legislation to a representative or senator. Organized outside groups may also help draft legislation. In fact, since the 1970s outside groups that advocate for specific causes called *interest groups*, also known as 'special interests,' have increasingly been sources of information for legislators when drafting legislation. Depending on the policy, they are also quite visible throughout the legislative process. It is very difficult to discuss the lawmaking process without mentioning interest groups. Research on U.S. Congress illustrates a mixed view of interest group influence on members, while research on state legislatures point to more influence on state legislators.[20] Interest group influence in state legislatures is exasperated in legislatures that are less professionalized and have term limits.[21] In term limited legislatures, there is a vacuum of institutional knowledge. Older members with a lot of experience used to mentor newer members in understanding and learning about the legislative process. Since interest groups are not affected by term limits, they have filled this role.

Lobbyists, individuals who represent an organized interest, are known to be permanent fixtures in the Missouri General Assembly. If one were to visit the Missouri statehouse, lobbyists are ubiquitous. They are hanging out in members' offices, attending committee meetings, and offering their expertise on issue areas. The number of registered lobbyists was about 978 in 2015, which makes them outnumber lawmakers 5 to 1.[22] It should be kept in mind that interest groups provide useful information and research to legislators. If they did not, they would not be used as sources again. Further, it is ultimately up to the representative or senator to introduce bills that are drafted by non-members to the assembly.

The member who introduces the bill becomes its *sponsor* and may seek to build a coalition for passage by gaining *co-sponsors*. A member becomes a co-sponsor when where two or more members sign on to support the introduced bill. This name applies to both U.S. Congress and the Missouri General Assembly. A bill with multiple co-sponsors may be a strategic way to garner support, especially if it is bipartisan. It is also a nice way to divvy up the work and illustrate broad support.

In U.S. Congress when a bill is introduced it goes to the presiding officer. It is then assigned a number and an 'H.R.' for House of Representatives or 'S' for bills coming from the Senate. The presiding officers are normally the Speaker of the House in the lower chamber, and the Presiding Officer in the upper chamber. These individuals play a very important and powerful role. They are of the party that has majority status. Why is this such a powerful position? They send the bills that are introduced in their chamber to committees to be worked on, which is called a *referral*. Committees are organized by subject areas and bills that are introduced are often sent to germane committees. Now, referrals may seem to be a just an administrative task for presiding officers, but, they can send these bills to any committee they would like. If they want to see the bill 'die,' then, they may send them to committees that do not have a much expertise in the subject area. This is a lot of power.

The Missouri General Assembly has a similar process with bill introduction and referral. However, there is one distinct difference. Before the bill is referred to committee, it is 'read' twice. The first reading is a formal application of a number and letter. "HB" is assigned to house bills and "SB" to Senate bills. At this point, the full bill is not read. The bill is then sent back in line for a second reading where majority party leadership, the Speaker of the House or President Pro Tem schedules it. Scheduling is another powerful role. This is because majority party leaders can delay the bill from being worked on by scheduling it for a much later date for a second reading. The second reading is when these two leaders refer the bill to a committee. Just as in U.S. Congress, committee assignment for bills can either streamline or stalwart a bill.

Another key difference between U.S. Congress and the introduction of bills are the types of bills that can be introduced. The U.S. Constitution prohibits any bills concerning appropriations to be introduced in the U.S. Senate. Bills with appropriations have to begin the process in the U.S. House. In the Missouri General Assembly, bills concerning appropriations can be introduced in either chamber. However, appropriations traditionally begin in the house.

3: Committee Work

Committees are where a majority of the work is conducted on a bill. In committee, the bill is worked on by examining the language, adding amendments, and hearing from a variety of citizens, interest groups, and other members of government about the pros and cons of the bill. Committees are organized along policy areas and sitting representatives serve on these committees. Assignments to these committees are made by the majority party leaders for both U.S. Congress and the Missouri General Assembly.[23]

Committee Room

© Yegor Korzh/Shutterstock.com

Generally, members who have seniority status receive their desired committee assignment. However, they can be stripped of their assignment or not receive their desired committee position if majority party leaders do not want them to. Desirability of these assignments may depend on the representative. Some representatives may want to serve on committees because it would serve their district well. If one comes from a district with a lot of farmers, serving on the Missouri House of Representatives' Agriculture Policy Committee makes sense. However, some may want a certain assignment due to its' prestige and the amount of attention they will receive through media. Attention helps incumbents with reelection as their name becomes more recognizable to constituents.[24] Some of the more prestigious committees include Appropriations in the U.S. House and both chambers of the Missouri General Assembly. These are considered to be prestigious because they deal with allocation of money and may garner a lot of media attention.

There are three different main types of committees, standing, joint, and conference. A *standing committee* is a permanent committee. The majority party can opt to reduce or increase the number of committees if they chose to do so. A *joint committee* is a committee made up of members from both the house and the senate. These types of committees are usually *select committees* that are not permanent and conduct *oversight* or investigations of government activities. A *conference committee* is a committee where members from both the house and the senate resolve differences in bills after the bill has passed with a majority vote through the house and the senate. A bill may not be in the same form if it originated in the house and then was sent to the senate to be worked on and vice versa. This is because it may have been sent through committee again and amended during the legislative process. The general forms of committees are similar when comparing the Missouri General Assembly and U.S. Congress. One difference is number of committees. The Missouri House of Representatives consists of 56 standing committees compared to 21 standing committees in the U.S. House of Representatives. The Missouri Senate has 18 standing committees and the U.S. Senate 21.

4: Getting the Bill out of Committee

After committees hear a variety of opinions from experts, citizens, or other governmental organizations they get to work on the bill. They utilize those hearings as well as research from their staff to work on the final language. At this point, they may have sessions in which they combine another bill to it, amend it, or rewrite it. By the time this is through, it may even be the case that it is not in the form the sponsors wanted it to be. After the committee is finished working on the bill, they vote to decide whether or not the bill will go to the floor of the chamber for debate. In the Missouri General Assembly, committee members make a "Do not pass" or "Do Pass" vote. A majority of "Do not pass" votes means that the bill does not make it out of committee. This really means that the bill 'dies' or is 'killed' in committee. A majority of "Do pass" vote means that the bill will go to the chamber to be scheduled for debate and voted on by members of the chamber.

5: Chamber Action and Floor Debate—Perfection

If a "Do pass" vote in committee succeeds, the next course of action is that the bill goes to the chamber for debate and passage. In the Missouri General Assembly, this process is called 'Perfection.' One difference exists between the House and the Senate for both the Missouri General Assembly and U.S. Congress. The house has a Rules Committee and the senate does not. Prior to the bill being scheduled it has to go through the Rules Committee. The majority of the members of the rules committee are traditionally majority party members. They set the rules or terms of debate. These rules can include time limits on the amount of floor debate, limits on the number of amendments that can be added to the bill, or no debate at all. The Speaker of the House usually directs the rules committee and may use this to strategically obstruct the passage of the bill on the floor. Rules may also be used to streamline passage.

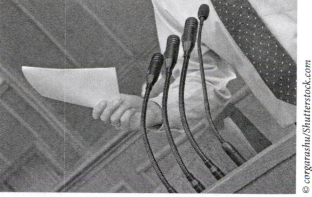

Floor Debate

The Missouri Senate perfection process is different from the house. It does not have a rules committee and has open debate. Like the U.S. Senate, much of the negotiation about the terms of debate occurs with members discussing it with the leader of the majority party. Since there are no time limits for debate, members of the U.S. Senate and Missouri Senate can *filibuster*. A filibuster means that a Senator can talk for as long as she or he likes until the bill dies on the floor. The threat of a filibuster by a Senator may be enough to alter the bills language in their favor. However, a key difference in the Missouri Senate is that a potential filibuster can be broke by *cloture* through ⅔rds of its' members voting to do so. In U.S. Senate ⅗ths of its' members have to do so. The U.S. Senate sets the bar a little lower in the percentage of senators it takes to stop a filibuster.

6: Final Passage

If a simple majority of members in the chamber in which the bill is being considered vote to pass it will go to the other chamber through this process. If significant differences in the bill exist after the bill has gone through the legislative process, then a conference committee works out those differences. Once the bill is in its' final form, both chambers perform a final floor vote for the bill to move to the executive to either sign or veto the bill. These methods are similar for both U.S. Congress and the Missouri General Assembly. One key difference, though, is the power of the executive in either signing or vetoing the bill. The Missouri Governor has a variety of veto options, while the U.S. president does not. These differences are discussed in Chapter 5.

★ Conclusion

The way in which the Missouri General Assembly functions is similar to U.S. Congress but has some key differences that make them unique from one another. This makes it part of a mosaic of state legislatures in the American political system. First, like most state legislatures, the Missouri General Assembly is much more reflective of the population demographics in the state. Even though, Missouri does better than U.S. Congress when considering the percentages of women and minorities that serve in the legislature, it ranks in the middle when comparing it to all states. Partisan composition too, is different than that of U.S. congress. Missouri has many more Republicans in the legislature U.S. Congress—which certainly reflects the partisan tide of the state.

Other key differences between the Missouri General Assembly and U.S. Congress include office professionalism, size, the number of terms, and requirements for office. Again, Missouri ranks in the middle in terms of office professionalism. It has shorter days in session, less pay for members as well as less full-time staff. The number of members is less than U.S. Congress, but more than other states such as California. Missouri is also a state that limits the number of terms for members of its legislative branch. It is one of fifteen states that have term limits. Additionally, the age requirements for office differ slightly. In Missouri, one has to be 24-years-old to gain office in the Missouri House of Representatives. Both U.S. Congress and the Missouri senate requires its members to be at least 30 years old.

★ KEY TERMS ★

Districts

Single Member Districts

Multimember Districts

Constituents

Delegate

Trustee

Lower Chamber

Upper Chamber

Redistricting

Malapportionment

Baker v. Carr

Term Limits

Incumbents

Legislative Professionalism

Part-Time Legislature

Citizen-Legislatures

Interest Groups

Sponsor

Co-sponsors

Referral

Standing Committee

Joint Committee

Select Committees

Oversight

Conference Committee

Filibuster

Cloture

★ ENDNOTES ★

1   Squire, Peverill, and Keith E. Hamm. 2005. *101 Chambers: Congress, State Legislatures, and the Future of State Legislative Studies.* Ohio State University Press.

2   Kurtz, Karl. 2011. "Declining use of Multimember Districts." The Thicket of State Legislatures. National Conference of State Legislatures. Available at: http://ncsl.typepad.com/the_thicket/2011/07/the-decline-in-multi-member-districts.html

3   Center for Women and Politics. Rutgers Eagleton Institute of Politics. See http://www.cawp.rutgers.edu/facts

4   U.S. Congressional Demographics obtained from: Congressional Quarterly Roll Call. 2015 Guide to the New Congress. (114th Congress). Available at http://connectivity.cqrollcall.com/get-the-ultimate-guide-to-the-new-congress/press. Demographics for U.S. State Legislatures and the Missouri State Legislature obtained from the National Conference of State Legislatures.

5   Ibid

6   See the Center of Women and Politics and the National Conference of State Legislatures.

7   Darcy, Robert, Susan Welch, and Janet Clark. 1994. Women, Elections, and Representation. 2nd Edition. University of Nebraska Press.

8   CQ Roll Call Guide to the New Congress.

9   See Bratton, Kathellen and Kerry L. Haynie. 1999. "Agenda Setting and Legislative Success in State Legislatures: The Effects of Gender and Race." *The Journal of Politics* 61(3) (August): 658–679. Also see Bratton, Kathleen A. 2002. "The Effects of Legislative Diversity on Agenda Setting: Evidence from Six State Legislatures." *American Politics Research* 30(March): 115–142. And Owens, Chris T. 2005. "Black Substantive Representation in State Legislatures from 1971–1994." *Social Science Quarterly* 86(December): 779–791.

10 Erikson, Robert S., Gerald C. Wright, and John P. McIver. "Statehouse Democracy: Public Opinion and Policy in the American States." Cambridge University Press, 1993.

11 Swain, Carol M. 1993. *Black Faces, Black Interests: The Representation of African Americans in Congress.* Harvard University Press: Cambridge.

12 University of Central Missouri, Politics and Social Justice Week. Senator Jolie Justus.

13 See Stiles v. Blunt, 1990. Also see Missouri Constitution, Article III Section 4.

14 See Kuhlmann, Robynn, "Statehouse Mosaics and the American Electorate: How State Legislatures Affect Political Participation" (2012). *University of New Orleans Theses and Dissertations.* Paper 1509.

[15] Recent research illustrates that despite populist claims, term limits have increased interest group influence and strengthened the executive branch in negotiating the state budget. See Kousser, Thad. *Term Limits and the Dismantling of State Legislative Professionalism.* 2005. Cambridge University Press: Cambridge.

[16] Squire, Peverill. 2007. "Measuring State Legislative Professionalism: The Squire Index Revisited." *State Politics & Policy Quarterly* 2 (Summer): 212–227.

[17] National Conference of State Legislatures

[18] Ibid

[19] See Also see. King, James D. 2000. "Changes in professionalism in U.S. Legislatures." *Legislative Studies Quarterly* 25 (May): 327–343.

[20] Kousser, Thad. *Term Limits and the Dismantling of State Legislative Professionalism.* 2005. Cambridge University Press: Cambridge. Also see Kousser, Thad. 2006. "The Limited Impact of Term Limits: Contingent Effects on Breadth and Complexity of Laws." *State Politics & Policy Quarterly* 6 (Winter): 410–429. and look at "congress and its' members"

[21] Ibid.

[22] Missouri Ethics Commission. Lobbyist/Principal Report. 9.26.2015. Available at: http://www.mec.mo.gov/lobbyist/lobbyistprincipal.pdf

[23] Although in state legislatures, the seniority status of these members do not have as much of an effect of getting on desirable committees or chair positions as U.S. Congress. See Squire and Hamm 2005.

[24] Fenno Jr., Richard F. 1978. *Home Style: House Members in Their Districts.* Boston: Little Brown.

Chapter 5

THE EXECUTIVE BRANCH: MISSOURI'S GOVERNOR AND THE U.S. PRESIDENCY

★ Introduction

In 2013, Missouri Governor, Jay Nixon, signed an *executive order* that defied Missouri's constitutional ban on same-sex marriage.[1] An executive order is a legal order by the chief executive (the governor) to state agencies. This particular executive order directed the Missouri Department of Revenue to allow same-sex married couples to file joint state tax returns. This flew in the face of the Missouri Constitution that was amended to ban recognition of same-sex marriages. Governor Nixon received harsh criticism from opponents and applause from supporters. Then, in the summer of 2015, the U.S. Supreme Court ruled in the court case of Obergefell v. Hodges that same-sex marriage bans were unconstitutional. Governor Nixon then issued another executive order to direct state agencies to comply with the Supreme Court ruling.[2] Meanwhile, in Missouri's neighboring state Kansas, Governor Sam Brownback also issued an executive order. However, Governor Brownback's initiative was different than Governor Nixon's. His executive order was based on what he considered to be religious liberty.[3] Governor Brownback's executive order prohibited state agencies from punishing religious organizations and clergy members if they refused services to couples based on religious convictions. These neighboring states had governors who were flexing their political muscle, but in very different ways.

Please go to the following link to see Missouri Governor Jay Nixon sign the executive order directing state agencies to recognize same-sex marriage after the U.S. Supreme Court ruled that same-sex marriage bans are unconstitutional: http://goo.gl/gbqlPN

Executive orders are one of many *implied powers* in the U.S. Constitution and state constitutions. Implied powers are the powers which are not explicitly listed in the Constitution, but assumed because comparable powers are listed. Similar to the U.S. president, governors have the role of executing the laws and directing agencies under the executive branch that handle governmental affairs. As the chief executive, these individuals are given the task of 'faithfully executing laws' born out of the legislature and court rulings. This *executive power* also includes appointment power—which is an explicit power listed in the federal and in state constitutions. Presidents and governors have the power to appoint heads of their respective agencies—which is a substantial amount of power. Important to note is that these powers differ between governors and the U.S. president.

Article IV of Missouri Constitution lays out the aforementioned powers and duties of the Missouri governor. For example, in Article IV, the Missouri governor is also tasked with being a guardian of the state—or "conservator of the peace throughout the state." This enhances the explicit power the Missouri governor has as the head of the National Guard. As an *explicit power*, a power that is listed in the Missouri Constitution, it allows the governor to deploy the National Guard. These powers will be discussed later in this chapter. Compared to other governors, the Missouri Constitution gives its governor a substantial amount of power. In fact, the Missouri governor has more tools in the form of a variety of types of veto's than the U.S. president does—which is a tool of *legislative authority*. This chapter is meant to give an overview of the differences and similarities between the constitutional powers of the Missouri governor and the U.S. president. The following sections will outline who these individuals are, where they come from, how they gain this prestigious political position, and their constitutional powers.

Governors: Who Are They?

Age, Citizenship, and Residency—Formal Requirements

Obtaining the presidents' or governor's seat is a difficult task. Elections for these positions are riddled with highly qualified and well-funded individuals who more than likely have been climbing the political ladder for quite a while. These seats are highly coveted and considered as one of the highest offices in the U.S. political system vested with a lot of power and duties. It is also very expensive to run for one of these seats. Governor Jay Nixon, for example, reportedly spent about 15 million dollars for his 2012 re-election campaign.[4]

Who are the individuals who make it to the states' highest political office? There are a couple of *formal requirements*, they have to meet. Formal requirements are conditions that are explicitly laid out in the Constitutions to hold the political office. Article IV of the Missouri Constitution requires that the governor should be at least 30-years-old to hold office. While some states have an age requirement of 18 years old, others have a threshold of 31 years of age.[5] Missouri's age requirement mirrors most states—33 states have a 30-years-old age requirement. Article II, Section 1 of the U.S. Constitution requires that U.S. presidents are a little older and sets the standard at 35 years of age.

Did you know?...

Kit Bond was the youngest serving Missouri governor. He was 33 years old when he began his tenure as governor in 1973. He also ran for and won the governor's seat again in 1981. At 33, Matt Blunt is the second youngest Missouri Governor—about 8 months younger than Kit Bond.

© 1976 Southeast Missourian Newspaper

Kit Bond running for governor

Residency and birth requirements also exist for governors and the president. The Missouri Constitution requires the governor to be a U.S. citizen for 15 years and a Missouri resident for ten years. Other states range from no state residency or U.S. citizenship requirements, to 20 years as a U.S. citizen.[6] This Missouri qualification for governor is actually quite stringent compared to other states. In fact, the residency requirement for the U.S. president is 14 years. However, the citizenship requirement for the U.S. president is that they have to be born a U.S. citizen.

Tenure and Term Limits

A long tradition in the United States for heads of states (governors and presidents alike) is to step down from their position after a short period of time. First U.S. president, George Washington, began this tradition by stepping down after serving two terms as the President—even though a limit on the number of terms, a president can hold did not exist at that time. Stepping down from the position as an executive is symbolic to the American political tradition. It illustrates that executives are not monarchs or seeking despotic power. Elections reaffirm that the power of choosing an executive is given to citizens. In fact, every U.S. president following Washington stepped down from office if they had served a second term, with just one exception. Elected in 1932, President Franklin D. Roosevelt was the only president that chose to run for reelection after serving two consecutive terms. Although President Franklin Delano Roosevelt won a fourth term, he died soon after being reelected. In 1951, the U.S. Constitution was amended with the 22nd Amendment. This created a formal limit on the number of terms for the U.S. presidency. Since then, U.S. presidents have been restricted to serve only two four year terms.

Just like the modern presidency, Article IV, Section 17 of the Missouri Constitution limits the number of terms a governor can serve to two four year terms. All states have four year terms, except two, namely Vermont and New Hampshire which have two year terms. Fourteen states have no term limits on the governor, which allows some governors to continue their tenure for as long as they decide to run and be elected.[7] Other states have limits on consecutive terms, so some can cycle back to the governor's office after a period of time. The Missouri Constitution does not allow ex-governors to run again after two four terms.

Informal Requirements for the Governor's Seat—Education, Occupation, Race, and Gender

Informal requirements for the governor's seat and the presidency also exist. *Informal requirements* are consistent characteristics that office holders have in common and therefore are considered as factors that help candidates win. They are not hard and fast formal requirements as laid out in the United States and state Constitutions. They are trends consistent with gaining elective office. Some informal requirements involve having a certain level of education and prior political experience. Almost all modern day governors, at minimum, have a bachelor's degree. Most have postgraduate education, mainly in law.[8] Prior political experience, especially a statewide elected position, is very common.[9] These individuals have climbed the political ladder by having experience in holding lower level elective office. Some have prior experience holding federal seats such as in the U.S. House of Representatives or the U.S. Senate. It is rare that a candidate with little to no political experience may get through the electoral thicket and win the governor's seat. More recently, candidates with little to no political experience were high profile individuals in the first place. Former California governor Arnold Schwarzenegger and Minnesota's former governor, Jesse 'the body' Ventura are such examples.

Governor	Years of Service	Education	Occupations Prior to being Governor
Jay Nixon (Democrat)	2009–2016	B.A. Political Science, J.D.	Attorney, Missouri State Senator, Attorney General
Matt Blunt (Republican)	2005–2009	B.A. History (U.S. Naval Academy)	Naval Officer, Missouri House Representative, Secretary of State
Bob Holden (Democrat)	2001–2005	B.A. Political Science, Graduate level executive courses at Harvard	Missouri House Representative, State Treasurer
Mel Carnahan[11] (Democrat)	1993–2000	B.A. Business, J.D.	Attorney, Missouri House Representative, State Treasurer, Lieutenant Governor
John Ashcroft (Republican)	1985–1993	B.A., J.D.	Attorney, State Auditor, Attorney General
Christopher "Kit" Bond (Republican)	1981–1985; also served from 1973–1977	B.A., J.D.	Attorney, State Auditor
Joseph Teasdale (Democrat)	1977–1981	B.A., J.D.	Attorney
Warren Hearnes (Democrat)	1965–1973	J.D.	Missouri House Representative, Secretary of State
John Dalton (Democrat)	1961–1965	B.A., J.D.	Attorney, Attorney General

© VOLODDYMYR V. MARTSENIUK/Shutterstock.com

Harry S. Truman, who served as Vice President to Franklin D. Roosevelt, is the first and only U.S. president from Missouri.

Those who have served as Missouri governor reflect the general informal requirements discussed above. Since the 1860s, all Missouri governors have had a college education, a law degree (J.D.), or an equivalent background in law. Table 1 illustrates that the last ten Missouri governors had both a college degree and held a statewide political position. The last governor who did not have a substantial education was Governor Claiborne Fox Jackson in 1861. However, his tenure did not last very long. He only served for five months as governor before the state legislature removed him from the office. This was largely due to tensions between the legislature and the governor over the American Civil War.

The governor's seat is also a stepping stone to the presidency. In fact, more U.S. presidents have been governor than any other political position. This highlights how important informal requirements mean to gain the presidents' seat. Prior political experience seems to be a must for election. The only sitting president from Missouri was Harry S. Truman. He had prior political experience as a U.S. Senator, but never served as a governor. In fact, he gained his position as the U.S. president due to the death of President Franklin D. Roosevelt—he was Vice President during Roosevelt's tenure. Still, *Harry Truman* had a history of political experience and this mirrors the individuals who normally gain elective office as a governor and president.

Another informal requirement for state and federal executives in the United States includes race and gender. Most governors have been white and male. Similarly, the U.S. president had been consistently white and male until the election of an African American male, Barack Obama in 2008. This trend is similar for state governors. The trend was not broken until the election of Ella Grasso to the governor's seat in Connecticut in 1974—the first female governor.[12] Three women did hold a seat as a governors prior to Governor Grasso's election. However, they were not elected. They became governor because their husbands who were governor died, or was too ill to serve.[13] There has been an upward swing of women as governors that begun the 1980s. Since the election of the first female governor, there have been 33 women that have served as a governor. Nineteen of those were Democrats, fourteen were Republican.[14] As of 2015, six out of the 50 governors are women. Political party affiliation is distributed evenly among these women. Missouri has yet to elect a female governor, while neighboring state, Kansas has already had two female governors, Joan Finney and Kathleen Sebelius.[15]

Growth in the racial minorities serving as state governors has been slower than trends for women. From 1977 through 2007, during any given year, there were a steady number of one or two governors of color running the executive branch. No steady incline in the number of governors who were not white existed until 2009.[16] Generally, states that have high levels of minority populations have been characteristic of those states that have had a racial minority as a governor.[17] Hawaii is a great example of this trend. In Hawaii, the Asian American population is the highest in the country and its citizens have elected a few Asian governors. As of 2015, there were five governors of color. Still, in line with the current trend of many states, Missouri's governors have all been white and male.

Formal Powers of Governors

As discussed at the beginning of this chapter, governors and presidents have explicit powers. These powers are also known as '*formal powers*' which are explicit powers by virtue of their enumeration in the state or federal constitution. Formal powers can be for explicit or implied. *Informal powers* also exist. Informal powers are the powers that are extraconstitutional and contingent on a variety of factors. These include, personality, character, background, popularity, and resource structures in states. The following section surveys the formal powers of the Missouri governor and compares them to the U.S. president. The structure of the executive office, control over the budget, appointment power, veto power, and executive orders are discussed.

Elected Officials in the Executive Branch

One thing you might notice during presidential elections is that the candidates always have a running mate who would be their prospective vice-president. There is no separate box to check to elect the vice president of the United States. Whatever presidential candidate wins, their vice-presidential running mate also clinches victory and becomes part of the executive branch. This is not always the case with a state's equivalent—the *Lieutenant Governor* or any of the other executives in Missouri's executive branch. Each of the six elected executives in Missouri's executive branch are separately elected. This highlights the major difference between the federal executive branch and Missouri's executive branch. The president is the only elected official, with a vice president as a running mate. Missouri has a plural executive and these individuals can come from opposing parties of the governor. This system of a plural executive limits the formal powers of the governor as they do not have the authority to fire them. The duties of these other executives are laid out below.

Similar to the vice-president, the Missouri Constitution grants the lieutenant governor the authority to be first in line to succeed the governor in case of death, resignation, impeachment, or absence from the state. The lieutenant governor is also the presiding officer of the Missouri Senate. Like the vice president, the Missouri lieutenant governor also has the authority to cast a vote in the Senate to break a tie. However, unlike the vice president of the United States who steps down from office when the president's term is up, there are no term limits on the Missouri lieutenant governor.

Did you know?...

The Vice-President as the Runner-up

The original U.S. Constitution designated that the runner-up, or candidate that gained second place in the casting of electoral college votes would be the vice president. The last time a vice president obtained their position by being the runner-up was in 1800. This method revealed a flaw in the system. Both presidential candidates Thomas Jefferson and Aaron Burr tied in electoral college votes. Since U.S. Congress was charged with voting to break a tie, they ended up electing Thomas Jefferson. Congress voted 35-times to break this tie. Afterwards, the U.S. Constitution was ratified with the 12th Amendment to allow a running mate that would win the position of vice president.

There are other elected executives in the Missouri executive branch. These members may also be of the opposing party of the governor. Missouri has a *Secretary of State* whose job is record keeping, publication of state documents, and authentication of the acts of the governor. The Secretary of State also records and publishes election results, oversees the initiative process, and registers voters. The office of the Secretary of State also supplies applications for and validates individuals who seek to run for election if the seat represents more than one county. Finally, the Secretary of State oversees sections of the Missouri state commerce. This position is a four year term and elections for it are held at the same time as the governor and lieutenant governor, but, unlike the governor's seat, it is not term limited.

The *state treasurer* is also outlined in the Missouri Constitution. The duties of the treasurer are to keep the state money and invest the money which is not needed for state operations in order to gain interest on state funds. The office essentially serves as the state bank, and individuals in this office are limited to two four year terms. With money going out for state functions, who is responsible for oversight and making sure that state funds are used as outlined by law? This job goes to the *State Auditor* which is an accounting office. The state auditor is an independent watchdog of the treasurer and any office or public system that uses state funds. The state auditor is exactly what it sounds like. The office audits and takes a detailed look at how funds are used. The office also reports any mishandling of money as well as possible loopholes that may potentially lead to corruption. These reports are presented to the governor and the Missouri General Assembly. The auditor is elected during off-years which means that they are elected during election cycles outside of when the rest of the executive officers and state representatives are elected.

Lastly, the *Attorney General* is another statewide official whose main job is to legally represent the state. This is the state's lawyer and prosecutor. Their job is to prosecute violations in a variety of areas that constitute state laws. They will be the lead prosecutor and enforcer in issues concerning businesses and consumer affairs, environment affairs, criminal activities, and government affairs. They are also the chief legal advisor concerning interpretations of the state statutes and the state's constitution. However, the attorney general's prosecutions may be challenged of which the Missouri Supreme Court has that last say. As the state's legal representative, the attorney general serves as the state's representative when state laws are challenged. The attorney general is elected during the same election cycle as the governor has a four year term, and no term limit.

The Lieutenant Governor, Secretary of State, State Treasurer, Auditor, and Attorney General are all state-wide elected officials that make up the executive branch. Since they are separately elected, they may or may not come from the same political party as the governor. Historically, they are generally of the same political party. However, in 2015, two of the state executives were of the opposing party of the governor. These separately held elective offices can constrict the power of the governor—as it can be more difficult to direct the activities of the executive branch if there are differences in policy goals.

Gubernatorial Power

There are a variety of responsibilities and powers of the governor that are outlined by the Missouri Constitution. Despite the fact that other state executives hold a substantial amount of power in the branch, the Missouri Constitution grants a variety of powers to the governor. First, Article IV Sections 1 and 2 stipulate that "The supreme executive power shall be vested in a governor. The governor shall take care that the laws are distributed and faithfully executed, and shall be a conservator of the peace throughout the state." This means that, like the U.S. president, the governor has the power to control many of the state's agencies. It also gives the governor the power to setup commissions and reorganize the bureaucracy. As discussed in the beginning of the chapter, this clause gives the governor the ability to issue executive orders to direct state agencies. The main difference in this power between the governor and the U.S. president is that the Missouri Constitution, other statewide executives, and state laws restrict the governor from having broad control over agencies like the president does. The governor may have a constitutional provision to oversee certain agencies, but, is limited by other political entities that may also have the same jurisdiction.

The Missouri governor is designated as the "chief of the militia" and "may call out the militia to execute the laws, suppress actual and prevent threatened insurrection, and repel invasion."[18] This is an explicit power that makes the governor the *commander in chief* of the state militia—which is the National Guard. Along with the power of being the 'conservator of peace' this gives the Missouri governor the broad power to call up the National Guard when there are civil disturbances and/or natural disasters. More commonly, the National Guard is utilized for disasters such as destruction caused by tornadoes and flooding. These men and women are used to help allocate resources to those in need

The Missouri National Guard can be sent by the Missouri governor during times of crisis such as the Joplin tornado and civil unrest in Ferguson, Missouri.

after a disaster. Although calling up the National Guard for civil unrest is rare, Governor Jay Nixon more recently deployed them in 2014 to support local law enforcement in Ferguson, Missouri.

Like the U.S. president, the governor of Missouri has *appointment power*. However, there exist many stipulations on appointments for the Missouri governor. The governor appoints individuals to public office in case of a vacancy, unless otherwise provided by law.[19] These types of appointments in Missouri history are fairly rare but can occur. More recently, when State Auditor Tom Schweich committed suicide, Missouri Governor Jay Nixon appointed Nicole Galloway to fill the vacancy until the next election. Other appointments include the power to appoint the heads of executive agencies. Like the U.S. president, appointments made for the heads of executive agencies are only confirmed with the *advice and consent* of the Missouri Senate. When it comes to members of administrative boards and commissions, the governor's appointment powers are quite limited. Some have set terms for members that limit vacancies when newly elected governors come in to office. Others may have stipulations that a certain amount of democrats and republicans serve on them. These certainly limit the governor's ability to place the people he or she prefers for most of these positions. A survey of the appointment power of the Missouri Constitution easily illustrates that most of the appointments are limited and have to be confirmed by the Missouri Senate.

Legislative Powers—Control over the Budget and Veto Powers

Although appointment power is limited, the budgetary power of the Missouri governor's is quite strong compared to the U.S. president. Both the president and governor submit a budget to their respective legislatures and both are restricted by spending on items that are dedicated to programs which are mandatory by law. Article IV, Section 24 of the Missouri Constitution requires the governor to submit a budget to the General Assembly. A powerful mechanism emerges out of this process. The mere fact that the governor submits a budget to the legislature gives the power of setting the agenda. Further, Article IV, Section 27 gives the Missouri governor the power to control spending in the state. This means that if state revenue, or income, looks as if it may cause a shortfall, the governor can withhold funds.[20] This is a power that president of the United States does not currently have. The 1974 Impoundment Control Act made any withholding of funds by the president subject to congressional approval. A similar amendment to the Missouri Constitution was approved by Missouri citizens in 2014. Missouri's Constitutional Amendment 10, places some restrictions on the Missouri governor from withholding funds.

Another agenda-setting power for the Missouri governor is what is similar to the president's *State of the Union Address*. Article II, Section 3 of the U.S. Constitution states that the president shall give to Congress information on the state of the union and recommend measures that the president thinks are necessary. This is when presidents try to set the agenda with Congress and is one way to influence the type of legislation they work on. Over time, it has become traditional to address Congress through the State of the Union address—which garners much media attention. Similarly, the Missouri Constitution reads almost exactly like the latter section of Article II of the U.S. Constitution. Article IV, Section 9, states that the governor shall give to the Missouri General Assembly the state of the government. This is known as the *State of the State Address*. The State of the State Address is now broadcasted on television at the beginning of the legislative session every January. This also helps the governor set the tone for upcoming legislation. But legislative power does not stop there. The governor closely monitors the legislature with staff who attends meetings and debates. Of course, the governor and staff can also write legislation and have a representative or senator introduce it on the executive's behalf.

Both the U.S. president and all governors have the power to *veto* legislation. A veto is the ability to reject legislation that has been passed by the legislature. U.S. governors, by far, have more veto options in their arsenal than the U.S. president. What does this mean? Many people think that a veto is solely the ability to reject the full piece of legislation. This is not always the case. There are a couple of types of vetoes. First, a *full veto* rejects the entire legislation that comes to the executive's desk. Both U.S. presidents and governors have this option—including the Missouri governor. The U.S. president is restricted to utilizing the full veto.[21] For a brief period, President Clinton utilized the *line-item veto* which is the ability to veto specific lines in legislation while approving the rest of it. This was ruled unconstitutional by the U.S. Supreme Court. However, 45 states allow governors to line-item veto in some form or another, but most are restricted to bills concerning appropriations.[22] Missouri's governor has the power to line-item veto, but, only on appropriations. One caveat is that the Missouri governor cannot reduce public funds for schools or payments for public debt.

Override Sessions

One of the checks the legislature has on the executive branch is the ability to *override* vetoes. Overrides of vetoes for both the U.S. president and Missouri governor require two-thirds of a vote from their respective legislatures in both the house and the senate. Overrides from U.S. Congress may occur from none to fifteen times over the tenure of the president. Historically, overrides by the Missouri General Assembly had been few and far between—less in occurrence than U.S. Congress. However, Governor Jay Nixon faced a 'veto-proof' legislature after the 2012 election. It was historic when two-thirds of both the house and the senate constituted that of the opposing Republican party. Afterwards, this veto-proof Missouri General Assembly overrode 58 pieces of legislation that Governor Nixon had vetoed. This was a historic session. The last largest override session was in 1833 with 12 pieces of vetoed legislation overridden. The 2015 legislative session marked Governor Nixon as the most overridden governor in Missouri history. Indeed, if the governor faces a veto-proof legislature, the power of the veto becomes relative.

★ Conclusion

Although the duties of chief executives, the U.S. president and state governors, are similar, it is certainly the case that their offices can differ in requirements, structure, and power. The individuals who gain these positions are required to be older than the requirements set by state legislatures. Informal requirements have been that they are educated, have held prior political office, and that they are white and male. However, this trend is slightly changing. Females and racial minorities have been gaining ground in the governor's seat; while there has never been a female president.

The structure of the gubernatorial executive branch is different than that of the presidency. Governors often face separately elected officials that make up their branch. This form of plural executive does not exist for the president. Another difference is that state laws often confine governors from having the amount of control over state agencies and commissions that the president does not have. Although appointments to positions require senatorial consent for both the governor and the U.S. president, many appointments are restricted or overlap the tenure of Missouri governors. However, budgetary power and veto power of state governors, including the Missouri governor, is stronger that the U.S. president. The Missouri governor can withhold funds and line-item veto while the president cannot. Even though a more recent constitutional amendment has restricted some of this power, the Missouri governor still has more veto options than the U.S. president.

★ KEY TERMS ★

Executive Order
Implied Powers
Executive Power
Explicit Powers
Legislative Authority
Formal Requirements
Informal Requirements
Formal Powers

Informal Powers
Lieutenant Governor
Secretary of State
State Treasurer
State Auditor
Attorney General
Commander-in-Chief

Appointment Power
Advice and Consent
State of the Union
State of the State
Full-Veto
Line-Item Veto
Override

★ ENDNOTES ★

1   Missouri Executive Order 13–14

2   Missouri Executive Order 15–04

3   Kansas Executive Order 15–05

4   Associated Press. Missouri Governor Nixon Spends $15.5 Million on Reelection. December 6th, 2012.

5   The Council of State Governments. The Book of the States 2014. Table 4.2, pg 151.

6   Ibid

7   The Council of State Governments. The Book of the States 2014. *Constitutional and Statutory Provisions for Number of Consecutive Terms of State Elected Officials. Table 4.9, pgs 164–165.*

8   See Donovan, Todd, Daniel A. Smith, Tracy Osborn, and Christopher Z. Mooney. 2015. "State and Local Politics: Institutions and Reform." Pgs 266–267. Cengage Learning: CT.

9   Ibid

10 Information was gathered through the National Governor's Association, former governor's official websites, and Project Vote Smart.

11 Note: Lt. Governor Roger Wilson became Missouri's Governor after Mel Carnahan died in a plane crash. Wilson served until Bob Holden was inaugurated.

12 Note: First female governors were not elected…

13 See Center for American Women and Politics, Eagleton Institute of Politics, Rutgers University. History of Women Governors. Available at: http://www.cawp.rutgers.edu/history-women-governors

14 Ibid

15 Information was obtained by searching the National Governor Association's former Governors bio's.

16 See Donovan, Todd, Daniel A. Smith, Tracy Osborn, and Christopher Z. Mooney. 2015. "State and Local Politics: Institutions and Reform." Pg 270, Figure 8.5 "Number of Elected Women and Non-Anglo Governors Serving 1975–2013. Cengage Learning: CT. Also see the Kurtz, Karl. 2009. National Conference of State Legislatures. The Thicket of State Legislatures. Racial and Ethnic Minority Governors. With Credit to Christopher Z. Mooney.

17 Donovan, Todd, Daniel A. Smith, Tracy Osborn, and Christopher Z. Mooney. 2015. "State and Local Politics: Institutions and Reform."

18 Article IV Section 6, Missouri Constitution.

19 Article IV Section 5, Missouri Constitution.

[20] The Missouri Governor can only withhold general revenue funds.

[21] There was a brief period of time when the U.S. President could line-item veto. This was due to the Line Item Veto Act that was passed by Congress and signed into law by President Bill Clinton in 1996. In 1998 the Supreme Court struck down the act ruling that it was unconstitutional under the Presentment Clause of the Constitution in the court case Clinton v. City of New York.

[22] See The Book of the States. The Governor's: Powers. Table 4, pages 154–155. Nation Governor's Association.

Chapter 6

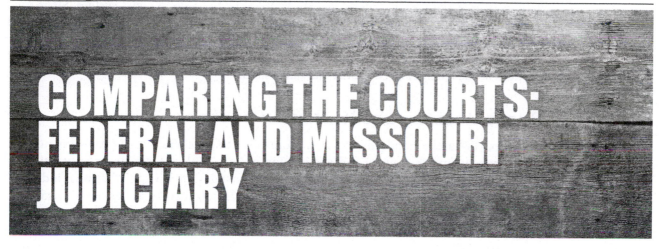

★ Introduction

In August of 2015, the Missouri Supreme Court announced their rulings on a series of challenges to state laws. One ruling was on the Mack Creeks Law which caps towns from generating more than thirty percent of their revenue from traffic violations. The Missouri Supreme Court rejected the challenge to that law which means that the state would keep those caps in place. The logic behind the law is to deter towns from relying too heavily on money from ticketing drivers for local government to function. Another ruling during that month also involved traffic tickets and the use of red light and speed cameras. The Missouri high court ruled that such ticketing practices put the burden of proof of innocence on citizens, which is unconstitutional. When citizens are accused of violating laws by the state, they are supposed to be assumed innocent first.

The latter are examples of the types of cases that may be reviewed by state court systems and can include a variety of issues such as the death penalty, abortion, and gun control. State judicial proceedings take on legal cases that cover crime, litigation between two entities, and the constitutionality of state laws. States' judicial systems are pillars of defining what state gov-

Missouri Supreme Court

ernment, citizens, and organizations can and cannot do. Along with state legislatures, they also set the terms of punishment if state laws are violated. The responsibilities of state courts are divided through the creation of legal **jurisdictions**, or the authority to make decisions or judgments over certain cases. The U.S. Constitution allows states to create and manage the states' judicial system—which means that the state of Missouri gets to handle legal cases that involve any question or violation of Missouri state law. This division through America's federal system of governance delegates powers to settle legal conflicts at both levels of government. This means that any question concerning state law is handled by states and violations or questions about federal law are handled by the federal court system. Since each state can create its own judiciary and the needs of the state vary due to unique issues and political systems, the structure of state court systems vary. The following section focuses on key similarities and differences in the jurisdiction, design, make-up, and selection of justices of the federal and Missouri judicial system.

Jurisdiction—The Missouri Courts

State courts handle hundreds of times more cases than federal courts. States handle all issues concerning the review and/or violation of laws. Unless a person or entity violates federal law, it is a military issue, a dispute between states, or a dispute between individuals who reside in different states if there is at least $75,000 at stake, states have jurisdiction over the legal proceedings. The structure of the Missouri court system is actually similar to that of the federal court system. Trial courts, a court of appeals, and a supreme court exist separately for U.S. federal government as well as Missouri. However, since most citizens are likely to confront a state law and not federal law, states handle most of the cases in the United States. High incoming caseloads are not uncommon. For example, in 2013 alone, Missouri had over 2.8 million incoming cases.[1]

Article V of the Missouri Constitution lays out the duties and jurisdictions of the state court system. Similar to the federal court system, there are two types of jurisdictions—original and appellate. *Original jurisdiction* means that the court has the power to hear a case first. Both the trial court systems and supreme courts have this power. *Appellate jurisdiction* is the power to review cases that have already been heard. The court of appeals and supreme courts have appellate jurisdiction. The court system functions to deal with disputes between individuals, determining the guilt or innocence of those who have violated state and/or local laws, and the protection of constitutional rights and liberties for citizens. Article V also lays out the administrative duties of the courts—which will be discussed later.

© Katherine Welles/Shutterstock.com

Explore the Missouri Courts at https://www.courts.mo.gov/civiceducation/pages/our_courts.html

Trial/Circuit Courts

Most cases are heard at the *trial court* level, also known as *circuit courts* in the state of Missouri. Trial courts establish case facts and decisions concerning the guilt or innocence of person as they apply to the law. Circuit courts have original jurisdiction over criminal and civil matters. There are 45 of these courts in the state of Missouri that serve its 144 counties. Most of the cases that go through these courts are not the quintessential movie-like trial proceedings that are often portrayed on TV or in movies. Most of them do not go through the jury phase where citizens serve to determine the innocence or guilt of the individual on trial. Most are *bench trials*. Bench trials are trials where guilt, innocence, or damages are adjudicated, or formally decided by a judge as the neutral party in the case. The federal court system also has a similar system called district courts. These are divided among 94 regions in the United States, and of course, only handle questions concerning violations of federal law.

Circuit courts play an integral role in handling the brunt of cases that are introduced in the state of Missouri. Since there are a variety of different types of cases, the Missouri circuit court system offers up a way to divide the labor through *divisions*. These divisions try criminal and civil cases and include ones pertaining to crimes among juveniles, municipal, probate, family, and small claims.

Did you know?...

Traffic Violations Load the Missouri Court System

Traffic violations are the highest number of cases that hit the Missouri court system. In 2013, it constituted about 78% of all incoming caseloads—this is 100-times more cases than criminal cases. Civil cases made up about 9.5% of all cases.[2]

Court of Appeals

When someone loses their case at the trial or circuit court level, they may try to challenge it by filing the case with the court of appeals. Both the Missouri and federal court system have an intermediate court between the circuit or district courts and the Supreme court. In Missouri, the appellate courts are called the Missouri court of appeals and in the federal court system, they are called the U.S. Court of Appeals. There are three Missouri court of appeals that are divided into three districts—Southern, Eastern, and Western districts. These Missouri court of appeals have jurisdiction over appeals that come from circuit courts within those districts. Similarly, the U.S. Court of Appeals are divided among thirteen districts and serve as an appeal system for lower courts within those regions. Thirty two judges serve on the Missouri Court of Appeals while ninety four federal judges serve the U.S. Court of Appeals.

Courts of appeal do not conduct their proceedings in the same way that trial or circuit courts do. Cases are reviewed by a panel of justices to review the constitutionality of the proceedings at the trial court level. The trial transcript is the evidence. Juries and witnesses are not utilized and three judges serve on the panel to review the case. Normally, the proceedings are such that the judges read the trial transcripts and question the attorneys representing the defendant and plaintiff of the original case. The Missouri Court of Appeals had about 4,000 incoming cases in the 2010.[3]

To see the jurisdictions of Missouri Circuit Courts and the Court of Appeals Jurisdictions explore these links: https://goo.gl/gyHKIA.

Missouri Supreme Court

Both the U.S. Supreme Court and the Missouri Supreme Court serve as *courts of last resort*. These courts have the last say in rulings concerning the lower court systems. This does not mean that the Missouri Supreme Court has the final say in all court cases. Since federal government has supreme power over state government, decisions by state supreme courts can be overturned—but only if challenged. However, the Missouri Supreme Court does have the last say when it comes to decisions out of the lower state courts or challenges to state laws that do not go through the lower court system.

© Niyazz/Shutterstock.com

The Missouri Supreme Court is the highest court in the state that is the court of last resort.

The U.S. Supreme Court and Missouri Supreme Court have both original jurisdiction and appellate jurisdiction. While the U.S. Supreme Court has nine justices, the Missouri Supreme Court has seven. Like the U.S. Supreme Court, usually the Missouri Supreme Court does not hear cases unless it has gone through the process of the lower court system. However, there can be exceptions. The Missouri Supreme Court has exclusive appellate jurisdiction over appeals cases that involve the death penalty, challenges to the right to hold a statewide office, the validity of U.S. treaties, the structure of state revenue, Missouri statutes, and the Missouri Constitution. Lower courts in the state cannot hear those cases.

The Missouri Supreme Court's job is to not only hear cases that may need review by the highest court in the state, but it also acts as administrators over the states' court system. The judges of the Missouri Supreme Court are responsible for the effective handling of cases throughout the entire state court system. They supervise the budget so that money can be appropriated for the proper functioning of the Missouri court system. Supervising the budget also means assessing where to allocate the money based on needs. There are a variety of workers in the court system that many may not think about when running a court system. For example, court recorders and a variety of employees are essential for its smooth functioning.

Sometimes, certain issues begin to put strains on courts. There may be an increase in number of drug cases, or some areas may need special attention such as mental health issues. It is also the job of the Missouri Supreme Court to organize the court system. When special issues strain the lower courts, or they determine that they need special attention, they may organize the system around them. Drug courts and courts that deal solely with mental health issues are such examples.

Judicial Selection and Qualifications for Service in the U.S. System—U.S. v. Missouri

Qualifications

Age, residency requirements, and terms of service for justices at the state and national level vary. Article III of the U.S. Constitution has no formal requirements for federal justices. However they must serve 'during good behavior.' Of course, the selection processes for federal justices has had a long tradition of choosing highly qualified individuals. Tenure for these federal justices are not limited, so they are lifetime terms. However, although rare, they can be removed from their positions because they are subject to impeachment by U.S. Congress.

Unlike U.S. federal judges, Missouri state judges have requirements to qualify for their position and these requirements can differ based on the division in which they serve. The minimum formal requirement for a municipal judge is that they must be a resident of Missouri and must be between 21 and 70 years of age. A law degree is not necessary to obtain the position. City charters determine the length of the term which municipal judges can serve. To cover legal education for these municipal judges, Missouri Supreme Court Rule 18 requires that municipal judges who do not have their law degrees earn more credits of continuing legal education annually than those who already have one.[4] Associate circuit court justices must be at least 25 years of age, a resident in the county they will serve in, licensed to practice law in the state of Missouri, and serve four year terms.[5] The bar for the age requirement is set a bit higher for circuit court judges. They must be 30-years-old, a resident of Missouri for 10 years, and have residency in the circuit division in which they serve. Circuit court judges serve four year terms.

Judges serving in the Missouri Court of Appeals must be 30 years of age, licensed to practice law in the state and must be a U.S. citizen for 15 years. Similarly, Missouri Supreme Court judges must be 30-years-old, licensed to practice law in Missouri, a U.S. Citizen for 15 years and must be a qualified voter in the state for nine years.[6] These justices serve 12 year terms and can apply for another 12 years of service once their term is finished. The mandatory retirement age is 70-years-old.[7]

Did you know?...

Challenging the Missouri's Mandatory Retirement Age for Judges

In 1991, the U.S. Supreme Court heard arguments challenging Missouri's mandatory retirement age for judges. Petitioners argued that the stipulation violated the equal protection clause of the U.S. Constitution and the 1967 Age Discrimination and Employment Act (ADEA). The U.S. Supreme Court ruled that Missouri judges were not considered 'employees' under the ADEA and that there was no distinction in their position between that of a judge and an elected or appointed official who makes public policy. Therefore the mandatory retirement age for Missouri judges is constitutional.[8]

Impeachment and Removal of Judges

Just as the U.S. Constitution provides oversight function for removal of justices through the Congressional impeachment process, the Missouri Constitution provides an oversight function as well. The reasons for removal from office for federal judges are actually quite obscure. As long as the judge serves "during good behavior," they cannot be removed. However, the Missouri Constitution more narrowly defines grounds for removal in Article VII, Section 1 which states that "All elective executive officials of the state, and judges of the supreme court, courts of appeals and circuit courts shall be liable to impeachment for crimes, misconduct, habitual drunkenness, willful neglect of duty, corruption in office, incompetency, or any offense involving moral turpitude or oppression in office." Only a handful of judges—six circuit court judges—have been removed from office in the state of Missouri.[9]

The process of impeachment can go two routes in the state of Missouri—through the Missouri legislature or an independent commission. The Missouri House of Representatives can vote to impeach judges. If the judge who the house assembly has sought to impeach is a lower court judge and not a Missouri Supreme Court judge, the trial would be heard by members of the Missouri Supreme Court.[10] In the case of impeachment of a Missouri Supreme Court judge, impeachment would be spearheaded by a vote in the House and the proceedings of the trial would be held by a seven person commission. In order to be impeached, five-sevenths of the supreme court or the seven person commission, depending on the type of judge, would be needed to remove them from office. If impeachment is not spearheaded by the legislature, an independent commission called the Commission on Retirement, Removal and Discipline (CRRD) can do so based on complaints filed with them. Created in 1972, the CRRD consists of six members with six year terms. These members include two lawyers appointed by the Missouri bar, two citizens appointed by the Governor, and two judges—one from the court of appeals and one from the circuit courts—appointed by judges in their respective jurisdictions. If the commission finds misconduct, then they can send their recommendations of disciplinary action to the Missouri Supreme Court for review.

Judicial Selection

One area that has yet to be discussed is how these individuals acquire their positions. The processes in which judges are selected in Missouri differ from the way U.S. federal government selects federal judges. The selection process of U.S. federal judges is based on recommendations of the states' U.S. Senators to the U.S. president's office. These recommendations stem from reviews from the American Bar Association. From there, the president recommends appointment of the judge to the U.S. Senate for approval. If approved, the federal judge is placed. The process of judicial selection in the state of Missouri is quite different than that of the federal level. Missouri is well known for the implementation of the *merit plan*, which will be discussed further. However, Missouri does not solely rely on the merit plan, it has a mixed system in which some judges can be selected through elections; not unlike elections for candidates running for political office, as well as through appointments. These selection processes usually are not without some controversy. The U.S. states have struggled with the selection methods of justices—and states have mixed systems depending on the level of the judicial branch—municipal, circuit, appeals, or supreme. The trick is to ensure that these judges are insulated from politics and outside influences. The merit plan was one way to deal with such issues.

One of the oldest methods of selecting judges was through *legislative appointment*. It means that state legislatures would choose judges to serve in their court systems. Most popular during the founding and post-revolutionary war period, legislative appointment was a reflection of the broad powers that the legislative branch used to have. Although two states still have this method, South Carolina and Virginia, the state of Missouri did not.[11] When Missouri was added to the union, judges were appointed by the governor with the advice and consent of the state senate—just like the federal judicial selection system we see today. In line with the early Missouri Constitution, states, namely, legislatures started to move on granting governors more power post-civil war in order to deal with rising complexities of the political system.[12] However, in 1849, Missouri moved in the opposite direction and placed selection upon citizens through electing judges via a popular vote. Today, only three states have that method. Ten states continue to have this second oldest method of selection, with some variation of either the legislature or a committee performing some sort of check on the governor.

Over concerns about political favoritism and the power of the governor's appointment method, Missouri moved to select judges via popular vote. The argument was that judges would then be accountable to the people of Missouri and not the politicos that selected them for the position.[13] For the most part, Missouri's selection method currently relies on *partisan elections* for municipal, associate, and circuit court judges. It means that these judges run for election just like any other political candidate. The exception to this rule is that circuit court judges in Clay, Greene, Jackson, Platte, and St. Louis counties and

Missouri's Supreme Court judges are selected under the merit plan.[14] Still, some municipal judges are selected by the appointment method via the mayor. Yet, combined, the most popular method of judicial selection is through partisan elections.

Partisan elections for judges had posed other probable issues with insulating judges from political forces or outside entities. One such issue that is currently up for discussion is whether or not judges can be swayed by the forces of popular opinion and the reliance on donors who keep their campaigns, and thus jobs, afloat. Some have argued that perhaps certain opinions such as desegregating the south may not have been cast, if for example the Supreme Court was subject to the whims of public opinion in order to keep their jobs.[15] More recently, the discussion has moved to whether or not judges may be more apt to side on cases where individuals or businesses have donated to their campaigns.[16]

The concerns over the amount of control politicos had over the judicial system led to a populist movement to amend the Missouri Constitution so that some judges, namely those serving on the Missouri Court of Appeals and the Missouri Supreme Court, are selected with a variety of 'checks.' These 'checks' involve the governor, legislature, and public input through a retention vote. This merit plan, or Missouri plan (also known as the nonpartisan court plan), was adopted in Missouri in 1940. Thereafter, it became one of the most popular judicial selection methods which other states have adopted.

"In an effort to keep justice 'blind', the Merit Plan was adopted in Missouri in 1940."

© Sign N Symbol Production/Shutterstock.com

There are essentially three steps to the Missouri merit plan when selecting Missouri Supreme Court judges. First, when a vacancy arises, a nonpartisan judicial commission is set-up which comprises the chief justice, three lawyers who are elected by the Missouri Bar Association, and three citizens who are selected by the governor. This commission reviews and selects three candidates to present to the governor. For appellate court judges, the panel is comprised of two lawyers, two citizens, and the presiding judge of the appellate district, selected in the same manner. The second step is that the governor appoints one of those three candidates to fill the position. That candidate then serves for a period of time and they go up for a *retention vote*. Finally, a retention vote is a vote by the citizens of Missouri to either retain or keep the judge in office, or to vote to select a new judge for the position.

★ Conclusion

The U.S. Constitution allows states to create their own judicial systems—thus creating a judicial system that varies within and between states. Further, much of the legal action occurs in states' courts as they handle more cases than federal courts. Missouri's judicial structure is similar to that of the federal judiciary. Although jurisdiction may differ over federal and state laws, the systems are similar in that both have lower courts, courts of appeal, and a supreme court. Some states do not have courts of appeals and in those cases, appeals are handled by the states' Supreme Court. Much of the difference between Missouri's court system and federal government's court system lays in the qualifications, tenure, and selection process. While Missouri has an age limit for service as a judge, the federal judiciary does not. Further, age differences in qualifications to gain office and the selection process differ at the municipal, circuit, appeals, and Supreme Court levels. In all, its design allows for the smooth functioning of application and challenges of laws in the state.

★ KEY TERMS ★

Jurisdictions
Original Jurisdiction
Appellate Jurisdiction
Trial Court
Circuit Court

Appellate Court
Supreme Court
Bench Trials
Divisions
Court of Last Resort

Merit Plan
Legislative Appointment
Gubernatorial Appointment
Partisan Elections
Retention Vote

★ ENDNOTES ★

1   See R. LaFountain, R. Schauffler, S. Strickland, K. Holt, & K. Lewis, eds. Last Updated 12 February 2015. Courts Statistics Project DataViewer, www.courtstatistics.org.

2   Ibid

3   See R. LaFountain, R. Schauffler, S. Strickland & K. Holt. *Examining the Work of State Courts: An Analysis of 2010 State Court Caseloads* (National Center for State Courts 2012)

4   See Supreme Court Rules. Rules governing the Missouri Bar and the Judiciary. http://www.courts.mo.gov/page.jsp?id=722

5   Missouri Constitution, Article V Section 21.

6   Ibid

7   Missouri Constitution, Article V Section 19.

8   Gregory v Ashcroft (1991)

9   Hardy, Richard J., and Joseph J. Carrier. Missouri Courts, Judges, and Juries. In Missouri Government and Politics.Eds., Hardy, Richard J., Richard R. Dohm, and David A. Leuthold. 199. University of Missouri Press.

10 Missouri Constitution, Article VII Section 2.

11 See the National Center for State Courts for current judicial selection systems in states. (ncsc.org)

12 Squire, Peverill and Keith E. Hamm. 2005. 101 Chambers: Congress, State Legislatures, and the Future of Legislative Studies. The Ohio State University Press: Columbus.

13 Hardy, Richard J., and Joseph J. Carrier. Missouri Courts, Judges, and Juries. In Missouri Government and Politics.Eds., Hardy, Richard J., Richard R. Dohm, and David A. Leuthold. 199. University of Missouri Press.

14 Missouri Constitution, Article V Section 19.

15 See Sandra Day O'Conner's Liberty Medal Acceptance Speech from the National Constitution Center. 2003 Available at: http://constitutioncenter.org/libertymedal/recipient_2003_speech.html

16 Canon, Damon M. 2007. "Justice for Sale? Campaign Contributions and Judicial Decision-Making." State Politics and Policy Quarterly 7(3) 281–297.

CPSIA information can be obtained
at www.ICGtesting.com
Printed in the USA
LVOW02s2003151216

517346LV00005B/15/P